Mr. C. & Me

CHRIS FORMAN

Copyright © 2021 by Chris Forman

All rights reserved

ISBN-13: 978-1-7773103-8-7

Published by Personal Sage Media
personal-sage.com

No part of this book may be reproduced in any form or by any electronic or mechanical means including information storage and retrieval systems, without permission in writing from the author. The only exception is by a reviewer, who may quote short excerpts in a review.

TABLE OF CONTENTS

Introduction 5

Unity 11

Generosity 21

Honesty 29

Vitality 39

Earth: Our Glorious Common Home 47

Wisdom 55

Sanctity 69

Cooperation 79

Integrity 93

Abundance 105

Balance 117

Choice 127

Love 135

The Future 145

About Chris Forman 157

Let's Stay Connected 159

A Free Gift for You! 161

Also Available in Paperback & eBook 163

INTRODUCTION

"That's it, Mr. Forman. You are *outta here*! Get your butt down to the office—I don't want to see you for the rest of the day!"

Ah yes, the office. 'Twas my veritable home away from home.

This is my third visit this week, I thought to myself. *Ms. Schmitts is just gonna love seeing my smiling face walking in the office again.*

I slowly sauntered down the hallway heading for the oh-so-familiar spot, my usual place of residence during my tenure in elementary school: the cold, stark, white wall just outside Principal Hikkling's office.

I knew they would not be happy to see me, again. I wasn't all that worried about it, though. Heck, it wasn't like three trips to "the wall" in a single week set a record or anything. My "personal best" was seven—yes, that's right, *seven*—friendly visits to my favorite hangout. I wasn't big on math back then, but even I knew that was an average of over one trip per day. You don't get those results without putting in some serious effort. Pretty impressive, eh?

So I trudged towards the office. I took my sweet time, of course, and tried to formulate a rationale for why I had been unjustly booted out of my grade 6 art class.

What will be my explanation this time? How will I explain how my classmate Bernie's fingers got glued together?

My predicament required a foolproof, persuasive explanation to reduce my culpability, painting me as an innocent victim in the whole deal.

The wheels in my twelve-year-old head turned and turned as I made my way down culprit's lane. I stopped for a quick drink at the water fountain. The cool liquid hit my lips, providing a fleeting moment of relief and distraction, some quiet before the inevitable storm.

I felt a familiar hand rest on my shoulder.

"Well, my young friend. What's the good word today?"

I turned around and beheld a sympathetic face looking down at me. It was Mr. Clifferd, the school's lone custodian (or janitor, as we called them back then). He gazed into my eyes with a knowing smile and emitted a soft chuckle.

INTRODUCTION

"Okay, my boy. Let's hear it. What happened this time?"

I practiced my pitch on Mr. Clifferd, developing it as I went. I told him all about the glue that I "accidentally" spilled on the table and the unfortunate cascade that led to Bernie's glued digits. I earnestly delivered my feverish account of the webbed fingers. Mr. Clifferd grinned, and with a wink said, "Sounds perfectly reasonable to me, Son. Could have happened to anyone."

I just *knew* he would understand. I felt better, comforted that at least *one* grown-up in this world truly "got" what it was like to be a perpetually misunderstood kid. Mr. Clifferd seemed to be the only employee at the school who consistently offered a sympathetic ear to the students.

Why can't all adults be like him? I wondered. *Why is it so difficult for adults to see the world from a kid's point of view?*

I continued down the hallway and reached the office just as the bell rang for recess.

No four-square for me today.
Again.

It's not an exaggeration to say that I spent nearly half my elementary school career in the hallway. To say that I was a mischievous boy is a bit of an understatement. I always felt that some rules were to be bent, if not outright broken.

As a kid, I couldn't embrace all the beliefs and values foisted on me by the teachers and administrators. They just didn't make sense.

Mr. Clifferd, on the other hand, seemed to understand my point of view. Whenever we shared our struggles and stories with him, he *really* listened. He made eye contact with us, looking at us like what we had to say *mattered*. He asked us our thoughts and opinions, validating our existence.

He gave my classmates and me the benefit of the doubt. He believed that at heart, we were all good kids. And he affirmed our goodness.

Mr. Clifferd wasn't particularly eloquent or well-spoken, yet he had a knack for knowing just what to say. All the students loved him, and we brightened whenever we encountered his warm smile. Mr. Clifferd was a real blessing in our lives. He was the best guidance counselor the school never had. Whenever I found myself in a real tough pickle (and taking the "walk of shame" down to the principal's office), I'd make a beeline for his "office"—the boiler room, to be honest—and tap on the door seeking his sage advice and encouragement.

Today, as an adult, I sure wish I could tap on that door once more. Especially today, as we all contend with the unprecedented challenges of navigating our way through the provocations of the COVID-19 pandemic.

INTRODUCTION

Here we stand, faced with a virus that continually seems to stay one or two steps ahead of us. People all over the globe are struggling to make sense of it all. The fear and anxiety that accompany such a threat weigh heavily on our spirits.

We sure could use some enlightened guidance right about now. Some sage advice to bring perspective, ease our concerns, and guide us to bring healing to the planet.

We need inspired direction. We need a compass to direct us to the way forward. We need minds open to new possibilities, and an awakened desire to *change* our behavior in real and meaningful ways.

This virus virtually demands a shift in our consciousness. An expansion of our perception. A rise in humanity's collective awareness.

If only Mr. Clifferd were here right now.

He'd guide us kindly and gently to make smart choices.

He'd help us discover and discern our own best course of action.

If only he were here.

UNITY

"Everyone hit the deck!"

The shrill voice echoed through the otherwise silent classroom. It was Alfie, my buddy and classmate. A passionate fellow who spent more time staring out the window than at the blackboard.

With an active tornado watch in effect, Alfie could not contain himself. He *lived* for moments like this.

"We're all doomed!" shouted Alfie. "Run for your lives!"

Now, if anyone other than Alfie screamed such dire warnings, we would have scrambled to the door and dove into storm position. However, the warning came from Captain Calamity himself, whooping at the top of his lungs. We had heard him cry wolf so many times that we had gone numb to it.

His previous warning involved a supposed UFO that flew over a giant oak tree in the schoolyard. Alfie had described in vivid detail the red laser beams blasting out of the front of the silver and blue alien spacecraft.

If anybody could quickly dream up a juicy drama, it was our one and only Alfie. Suddenly, a mind rattling crack of thunder. It was the kind you feel in your chest. The deafening pop was enough to startle even an inveterate storm lover.

"This is it! This is the big one! Here we go, guys!"

Alfie jumped out of his seat and scurried to the nearby window.

"Holy cow, you should see the sky out here! I've never seen anything so creepy."

Now, of all the wondrous events that occur in the natural world, I would have to say that thunderstorms are one of my favorites. The power and grandeur of lightning bolts illuminating the sky, followed by the deafening thunder, mesmerizes me. I can see the appeal of the storm chasing phenomenon.

I couldn't resist glimpsing the good ole southern Ontario cloudburst heading our way, so I joined Alfie at the window for a front-row look at the obliterating deluge heading our way. We pressed our noses against the cool pane of glass for a better look at the ominous sky.

"Whoa, man," I said. "You aren't kidding. Those clouds look totally freaky."

Alfie had a point. I had never seen anything like this before. The sky had a strange yellowish hue, and it bathed everything in sight with a bizarre golden glow.

"We're totally done for," whispered Alfie. "It was nice knowing you, Forman."

Crrrraacckkk!!!

Another jolt ripped through our eardrums.

B b b b b r i i i n g g g…. B b b b b r i i i n g g g…. Bbbbbriiinggg….

The ringing school bell now had our attention. But something was different. It wasn't the usual ring that started the day, signaled the end of classes, and announced our freedom after the last period. This ring had a different rhythm, but one we had heard before.

"TORNADO! It's a Tornado!!!" yelped Alfie, like a squawking chicken. "We're all gonna die!"

For once, Alfie's words accurately calibrated the collective mind in the classroom.

Growing up in Essex County, we had all practiced the tornado drill many times. We knew what to do in such a situation—we rehearsed it each year. However, this time was different. It wasn't a drill. This was *real*. It might actually be The Big One. The end. Our last moments on the planet.

"Okay, students, stay calm," said Mr. Ennz. Amid escalating fear, our teacher attempted to take charge of the class. He wiped a droplet of sweat that rolled down his forehead.

"Let's...all remember....to....to stay calm."

"Screw that!" Alfie cried. "I'm out of here!"

He high-tailed it across the classroom, out the door, and into the hallway. Talk about pure panic. The only other time I saw Alfie run so fast was when his mom chased him with a broomstick after he broke her favorite vase.

"Stu-dents...stu-dents." Mr. Ennz forced an unrealistic and exaggerated calm in his voice. No one was buying it.

"Everyone, proceed to the hallway. Remember, *single file!*"

Now, anyone who remembers tornado drills in the 1970s can predict what we did next. Someone in each classroom was responsible for opening all the windows because if a tornado rolls in, you want to make sure there is airflow between the inside and the outside.

I don't know if that recommendation still holds today, but in those days, it was common knowledge.

Unfortunately, that month it was Alfie's job to open all the windows, and he had already booked it and was likely hiding out in the closet where the cafeteria stashed the supply of chocolate milk and potato chips.

I was closest to the windows, so I jumped into action. As I pulled the handle on the window, I could feel the humid air blow forcefully into the classroom. The breeze felt moist and sticky, like stepping into a hot shower. The sultry air stuck to my skin, connecting my body to the natural phenomena brewing just outside the walls of our little elementary school.

The classroom emptied as I opened the windows. When I finished, I raced to the door and stuck my head around the corner to survey the situation. What a peculiar sight. All the students and teachers were crouched down on the cool tile. Bodies pressed up against the burnt orange lockers.

Everyone had their hands clasped over their heads. They looked as if they were ducking for cover, just like they do in those old western movies when the bad guy shoots up the saloon.

I spotted Mr. Clifferd as he came around the corner at the far end of the hallway.

"Everything's going to be just fine, folks," assured the janitor. "Breathe easy, stay still. This will all be over before you know it."

A school full of teachers and administrators, all in a panic. And the lone voice of reason and credibility—our beloved janitor.

I crawled on my hands and knees through the obstacle course of trembling, sweaty bodies to make my way to our trusted leader and friend. I sought reassurance that everything indeed *would* be okay.

"Holy smokes, Mr. Clifferd. What's going to happen to us?"

He glanced down at me.

"All is well, my young lad. You're going to be fine. Just relax and kneel down on the floor. The storm will pass in no time."

His composed, steady voice put me at ease. Even though I suspect he understood the potential gravity of the situation—the possible worst-case scenario, the chance of doom—he exuded a calm and courageous determination that settled my nerves.

I took his instructions and hunkered down on my knees, hoping that he was right and that this scary ordeal would soon blow over.

Bang...Boom...Ba Booooom....

More intense cracks of thunder roared from outside. Several girls started screaming. I felt my legs shaking. I closed my eyes and wished the storm would disappear.

I felt that familiar hand on my shoulder and opened my eyes to discover Mr. Clifferd right beside me, huddled down just like the rest of us. He looked over at me with affection. If this was The Big One, at least we would go out together.

The vulnerability of being clustered down on the floor, teachers and students alike, was a surreal experience. It was a strange sensation. A tangible feeling of nervousness and uncertainty swirled in the muggy air. It was as if we were ALL ONE, a collective entity, a unified consciousness.

A palpable communal awareness filled the sweltering hallway. We were present to the fact that we were in this together. Whatever was about to take place was going to happen to all of us.

Despite my closed eyes and pounding heart, I instinctively knew that I wasn't going through this alone. We were all clutching to the same raft in the same stormy waters.

In those tense moments, an indescribable awakening flooded into my already heightened perception. It was as if the walls of separation melted away. The electrified encounter with a life-threatening storm had united me with my fellow humans in the school in a way that made our supposed differences seem trivial and utterly meaningless. We were clearly experiencing this tempest together, like a single giant mass of terrified humanity curled up on the damp floor of the hallway —a messy and beautiful heap of humanity.

We were connected to the effects of the powerful thunderstorm. The loud rumbling of thunder, the steaminess of the air, the scent of perspiration and fear…there was no denying this was a collective ordeal.

In those frightening moments, we were *one*— with each other, and even with the storm. Nothing else mattered. Nothing else even seemed to exist. It was simply us, the walls of the school, and a looming cyclone merged into an inseparable reality. Where did the bounds of the storm end, and we begin? Where did humanity end, and the storm begin? The experience elicited an odd, yet paradoxically familiar, *knowing* that this was *how things really are* at the essence. Divisions between anything in existence were an illusion. A mind-blowing sense of unity pervaded my consciousness.

Have you ever experienced such a connection? A connection to *everything*?

If you have, you will understand exactly what I am sharing. The feeling is sublime, unforgettable, and almost beyond words. The mystics from various traditions who have walked this earth have tried to describe this phenomenon of oneness with all that exists.

Those moments tucked down on the floor awaiting annihilation provided a rare glimpse of a much bigger reality. It was a brief and remarkably powerful peek at a larger truth. For a few brief moments, the veil lifted.

We remain more intertwined with our fellow human beings and with the natural world than we realize. Heightened states of awareness provide a reminder that in this awesome universe, everything is interwoven into a giant, cosmic entity—an interrelated web of being that knows no bounds.

It is essential that we open our eyes and minds to this collective state of consciousness. The COVID-19 virus shouts a wake-up call, a reminder of the truth that ALL is connected. The complex

UNITY

matrix of all in existence links together in a marvelous waltz of being.

As we move forward in the days to come, it will serve us well to keep always in mind our undeniable interrelated relationship with all that exists. Our success as a species and as a loving consciousness demands that we continue to awaken to this potent truth:

We are ALL in this together.

GENEROSITY

"Wahoo! It's Hot Dog Day! And boy-oh-boy, am I *hungry*!"

It wasn't even lunchtime yet, and I could practically hear my classmate drooling behind me as he uttered his usual reaction to the boiled wieners that would enter his belly in forty-five minutes.

"I can smell 'em from here!"

Nobody got more excited about Hot Dog Day than Schmig Al. I swear, he lived for days like this. You could hear him smacking his lips, getting his stomach primed for the processed meat onslaught.

"I've got four of those babies coming my way," Schmig declared. "C'mon little doggies, come to Papa!"

The truth is, most students enjoyed Hot Dog Day when it rolled around once or twice a quarter. It was one of those sweet moments when we had a break from the usual peanut butter and jelly sandwiches and carrot sticks. Yes, Hot Dog Day meant the tuna fish and apple slices would wait until another day, as today was a special occasion. On Hot Dog Day, we even got to choose which potato chips and soda pop would accompany our glorious pink tube steak. We all enjoyed it, but it was a slice of culinary heaven for Schmig.

"I can't wait for my root beer and barbecue chips!" he announced to no one in particular. Rocking excitedly in his seat, he grabbed the back of my desk chair and shook it.

"It's almost chow time, Forman!"

"Take it easy, Schmig, will ya?" I responded. "You're practically bending my chair."

The aroma of steamy franks wafted from the cafeteria, down the hall, and now filled the room. Our stomachs grumbled in anticipation. Now being in Mrs. Grubb's class meant the culinary bonanza would be doled out in alphabetical order. Of course, you always started with the As, which resulted in Schmig getting his feeding time upfront.

"I sure am glad my last name starts with an A!" he triumphantly announced. "In my mouth and over my gums, look out tummy, here she comes!"

Have you ever seen a seagull devour a carton of French fries or a pigeon eat a bag of bread crumbs? They demolish the goodies in a matter of seconds.

Well, when lunchtime came, a similar phenomenon played out right before my very eyes.

As soon as those wieners hit his plate, Schmig Al was like a dog on a bone. If anyone's fingers came anywhere close to his mouth, they surely would wind up cleanly munched off. You'd think he hadn't eaten in a week. The frenzied sounds of weenie-chomping, chip-crunching, and soda slurping bellowed from his gaping maw. The gluttonous free-for-all was over in less than three minutes. (Yes, I actually timed it one day).

By the time I received my portion, Schmig had already annihilated his feast of frankfurters. There was nothing left but crumbs, condiment dribble, and some messy ketchup and mustard stained napkins. The ceremony was complete, save for the inevitable loud belch still to come from deep within Schmig's voluminous belly.

There I was, about to enjoy my meal, when Schmig grew unusually quiet. I suddenly sensed a pair of voracious eyes burrowing into my back. I knew exactly what was going down without even turning to look. After four wieners, Schmig was still hungry. He stared at my plate longingly, hoping I'd have pity and send some spoils his way.

I always had a soft spot for Schmig, big oaf that he was. He was full of life and a genuinely kind person. He stuck up for me once at recess, saving me from a black eye, or worse. He was the kind of kid you could depend on when in trouble.

So what if I hadn't even eaten half of my hot dog? So what if I only had munched a couple of chips? Schmig was still famished. I knew he would relish this noon-time treasure more than me. I could choose to look straight ahead, ignore those greedy eyes, and revel in my lunch. Or I could turn in my chair and offer to share with the kid who had saved me from the schoolyard bully.

This wasn't the only time this particular scenario played out. I had shared my food, including hot dogs, with Schmig several times before. It was always a delight to witness him gratefully accept (and inhale!) whatever scraps I shared from my midday meal. Sometimes it was leftover chicken from dinner the night before. Half a bologna sandwich. Or maybe even a chunk of my King Don. Inevitably, sharing always brought an incredible feeling of happiness and satisfaction in knowing my friend would thoroughly (if quickly) enjoy whatever I gave him.

This is the power of sharing. It's the experience of knowing that we spread gratification when we share the good things we have with members of our extended human family.

What if we *all* decided to choose one or two moments a day to choose generosity consciously—to share in some way with those around us?

GENEROSITY

We've all heard stories of someone perhaps at a toll booth or drive-through paying for the person in line behind them. Indeed, we've all been the recipients of someone's "random act of kindness" at one time or another. And we may have similarly blessed others on occasion. Just imagine what kind of world we could create if everyone practiced generosity *habitually*, as a way of life—a way of *being*. Imagine a planet of people who recognized we *are* our brother's keeper. Imagine if everyone shared an understanding that when we bless others, we doubly bless ourselves.

Surely, you've heard of the "hippie" movement of the 1960s and 70s. Perhaps you were even a part of it? Well, the hippies wanted to change the values of society. They desired to live in a civilization that encouraged people to share their possessions, talents, and ideas. The hippies devoted themselves to this new way of being, offering their energy and spirit to a communal and equitable approach to living. There was a powerful sense of belonging and family amongst the believers. They experienced a profound sense of fulfillment and connection in their mutual exchanges. Whether someone needed a ride, a place to crash, or a meal to fill their stomach, a fellow hippy would provide what they could.

What an awesome, loving world the hippies tried to arouse: a place where everyone could contribute whatever skills, sentiments, and gifts that they had, in full trust that their gifts would be honored and in some way reciprocated.

The hippie movement envisioned a culture of trust and sincerity. They craved a global community reflecting a belief in solidarity and mutual goodwill. Some even chose to live in communes, striving to live in harmony with each other and nature. They enjoyed a collective sense of responsibility; everyone's contributions were valued and valuable.

Can you imagine what humanity could attain if we decided to take a more determined approach to *living with* each other? Can you imagine experiencing a connected feeling of community on a daily basis? A collective interdependence? A broad appreciation of our obvious similarities?

As I write these words, I am looking out the window and noticing all the activity happening just beyond my backyard. A couple of neighbors are cutting their grass. One person is running his weed whacker. Another neighbor just pulled into her driveway and she's unloading bags of groceries from the trunk of her car.

The thought occurs to me: *what if my neighbors decided to share a lawnmower? Would my neighbors be willing to share a single snowblower for the neighborhood? What if we agreed to loan out, or borrow, tools required to complete a quick fix? Could we utilize the collective resources we possess to benefit everyone?*

I wonder how many people still take advantage of their local library? These days it's more common for people to go online. It turns out, the internet is an incredible method of sharing information and ideas. The local library is an analog equivalent. In fact, in addition to the many physical resources available for check-out, most libraries nowadays offer free computer and internet access—the best of both worlds. The whole local area can prosper when its residents are able to access a common source of wealth and connection.

As we emerge from the global pandemic, places that foster community will be essential in drawing neighbors closer together. We can *all* benefit from a collective willingness to share whatever we can bring to the table of life.

Just as it was easy for me to share my lunch with Schmig when I turned my focus to the gratification it would bring him, it's just as simple to offer to the world whatever generous contribution you can offer. A planet of inhabitants who choose to spread their blessings would provide a sight worth beholding.

We can *all* make this a reality if we *choose* to make it a priority. The more people who jump on this train of loving possibility, the more we can actualize this new way of living and being.

Let's make a conscious resolution to discover a better way to be a part of the human family. Let's commit to offer whatever we can to ensure the mutual success of our fellow humans.

For some readers, this may all sound too lofty or idealistic. Okay, fair enough. Let's keep it super practical and achievable. Forget about changing the world. Instead, focus on changing your neighborhood. Start with you. And your neighbors. Not the ones half a world away, but the ones who live on your street, next door, and around the corner.

Be *that person*. The one who is willing to—and actually *does*—share their resources for the benefit of others. It has to start with someone. Why not you?

This is how we can initiate a generosity revolution.

One *person* at a time.

One *act of generosity* at a time.

Starting with *you* and *me*.

Starting *today*.

HONESTY

Whaaack! The loud crack of the strap hitting the principal's desk ripped through our eardrums. The sound was both startling and unforgettable.

Whaaack!!

The second strike—just as deafening, just as scary.

"Okay, gentlemen. Who's ready to talk?"

Mr. Hikkling stared into our eyes, looking for a tell of fear, vulnerability, or weakness.

"Who is brave enough to tell me what the heck happened yesterday?"

None of us moved an inch, our mouths firmly shut in nervous alliance. We knew precisely what had gone down the day before. But there was *no way* we were going to confess.

Craaack!

The hard rubber switch smacked off the desk again, this time with even more intensity. It looked like a giant piece of saltwater taffy, the kind you would get at the local fair every summer. It was a reddish color with a thick, black stripe running down the middle.

Craaack!!

This one was terrifying. The principal's face was beet red and angry.

"Well, boys, what's it gonna be?"

It was getting serious. The three of us had never seen Mr. Hikkling so enraged. We were on the brink of certain catastrophe. The veins on his furious forehead swelled like they were going to explode. We knew that if someone didn't speak up soon, a painful blow to the hand was coming our way.

"I'm going to give you guys five more minutes to come up with an answer!" He rose out of his chair and stormed out of his office, slamming the heavy wooden door behind him.

"Holy moly, did you see that thing?" Dugg whispered. "We better fess up."

"What do you mean w*e*?" said Dezzi. "I can't believe I'm in this mess. My mom is gonna kill me."

I had never seen these two so panicked. We had each spent plenty of time in the principal's penalty box. But something felt different this time, and we faced a hard decision.

Dugg's voice quivered as he spoke, "We gotta come clean, guys. I think he really means it this time!"

"I'm not saying anything!" barked Dezzi. "If anyone should be talking, it's *you*, numbnuts!"

I needed to intervene and say something to calm the two of them down, "Just stick to the plan, guys, and everything will be okay." And after a brief pause, I added a qualifying, "Probably."

"*Probably?* Have you lost your mind, Forman?" Dugg protested. "He's gonna whack us until we pass out!"

We had heard rumors of students getting the strap from Mr. Hikkling. Tales of torture and extreme agony. It was the early 80s, after all. Schools could get away with this stuff back then. Kids and students had fewer rights than they do today. Until misery and terror loomed large. *What's our best move?*

"Hair on the hand?" I asked my companions. It was a risky move, but perhaps the only one that might foil the principal's punishment.

"Yeah, let's do it!" said Dugg. "Dezzi, we'll use your hair. It will work best."

We referenced the long-held legend of the "hair on the hand" trick.

Within the hallowed halls of our elementary school existed a dubious, yet firmly held, belief that if you placed a simple strand of hair across the palm of your hand just before you got hit, the strap would strike the hair and slice right through your skin, cutting your palm wide open.

If the trick worked, blood would gush out of the gaping wound and squirt all over the walls of the office. With such grotesque and irrefutable evidence of abuse in your favor, you could then reach for the phone and call your parents to report the crime. They'd rush to the school, then call a lawyer, and you could sue the school for a million dollars. Instead of perpetrator of a petty crime, you'd then rise to brave victim and whistleblower who exposed a culture of abuse. Despite the accompanying pain of laceration, considering our circumstances, it seemed like an attractive possibility. Perhaps the only move we had left.

The thick oak door swung open, and our tormentor appeared. He sat down in his chair, a menacing scowl clung to his sweaty face.

"Alright, gentlemen! Time is up. Let's hear it."

Despite our previous silence and protests of innocence, we knew all about the smoke bomb thrown into a math teacher's car. It had not only stunk up the inside of the vehicle as intended, but it also burnt a small hole in the passenger side carpet.

An eyewitness to the incident reported it to the school's secretary, along with the names of the alleged evildoers: Dugg, Dezzi, and Forman. The witness wasn't wrong.

Should we tell the truth about the events in the parking lot and endure an inevitable beating from the Belt of Destruction?

As I asked myself that question one more time, a distinct memory filled my awareness. It was Mr. Clifferd advising me that honesty is the best policy, especially when it matters most.

"Tell the truth, my boy!" Mr. Clifferd had said. "If you want to succeed in the dance of life, you have to face the music."

His sound, but difficult, advice filled me with the confidence to speak up.

"Well, sir, it's sorta like this," I began. "We know what happened yesterday. And we can see that you're really mad about it. The truth is, sir, all three of us are to blame. What we did yesterday was a bad decision, and we're very sorry about it. We know we're in trouble. You can do whatever you want, of course. Please just realize that we meant no harm. It was a practical joke gone bad."

The words hung in the air for what felt like a painfully long time.

What was going to happen? The strap? Suspension? Expulsion? All of the above? We were at the mercy of Mr. Hikkling.

What happened next took us all by surprise. Our principal leaned forward in his chair and peered into our jittery eyeballs.

"Listen up, boys. I am sorely disappointed in your behavior. You all know better, and I sincerely hope you've learned a valuable lesson. I appreciate your apology and taking responsibility for your actions. Now, go back to class, and we will deal with this tomorrow."

Whew! What a relief!

He spared us the corporal punishment we so feared. We had escaped complete and utter disaster. In the end, we received two weeks of detention plus a month of clean-up duty out in the schoolyard.

I'll tell you this much: having to stay after school for a few weeks and picking up empty chip bags and chocolate bar wrappers was a heck of a lot better than getting beaten with a torture device. Besides that, no expulsion. No involvement from the local police. It could have been much worse, considering that hole in the carpet.

We were grateful for the reprieve, and I was so thankful I had remembered Mr. Clifferd's counsel, to tell the truth.

Those tense moments in the principal's office opened our eyes to the value of honesty and of taking responsibility for our behavior and choices.

It's time for us to take a long, hard look at ourselves in the mirror and examine our relationship with telling the truth. A commitment to the revealing light of honesty can illuminate our paths to a better way forward.

Taking Mr. Clifferd's advice ("Tell the truth, my boy!") will not always feel like the best option. It's certainly not the path of least resistance. Being candid with yourself, let alone others, can cause discomfort. Sometimes the forthright road appears onerous, if not downright scary. We've all had moments in our lives where making an honorable choice required a heroic share of courage.

The COVID-19 pandemic shows us the imperative of honesty. The virus does not care if we regard the truth as bothersome or a breeze. It doesn't concern itself with our tendency toward self-denial, or our hesitation to make the right call in a challenging situation.

Look, a lot of what we have to contend with nowadays just plain sucks. A lot of people hate wearing masks. (I mean, who likes it?) Many of our favorite shops and restaurants are still shut down. Some of them will never re-open. It now takes significant effort just to socialize.

I'm not commenting on the efficacy of the measures put in place to stop or slow the spread of the virus. My point is that it ain't always smooth sailing in this life, and when the waters get rough, it's vital to navigate the stormy waves with a trustworthy compass.

Seeking out and selecting the honest approach will always serve you well. Knowing that you chose the high road provides a strong sense of assurance and freedom of conscience and spirit.

The positive future we wish to create requires being real with each other. It demands that we authenticate our approach to living. Whether it's a viral attack, a climate change challenge, reckoning with our health, or any other curveball that life throws our way, it's best to stare it straight in the face.

Isn't this what we want for our children? Don't we want them to live in an open, sincere society? Wouldn't it be amazing if we all decided to "tell it like it is"? No more games, no more deceit, no more betrayal: just a simple commitment to the simple truth.

When I spoke up that day in Mr. Hikkling's office, it felt terrifying at first. As soon as I spoke, it felt liberating. As the saying goes, the truth shall set you free. Guileless actions bring their own rewards.

It may seem overwhelming at times, and maybe a bit nerve-wracking, but believe me when I say that reckoning with the truth is always the best option, no matter what dark clouds come to call.

Can you imagine if the leaders of this planet chose to be straight up with each other, and with us?

Wouldn't it be a relief to our fellow human beings, and to the earth itself, if we simply told the truth?

We could make huge strides in confronting the challenges of our times. Imagine, if we merely resolved to reconcile ourselves to the plain truth, what strides we could make in solving issues such as racism, sexism, poverty, homelessness, pollution, and inequality.

Our future as a species is crying out for this new state of being. We are awakening to a new and profound way of interrelating with each other and this awesome spinning chunk of rock that we share.

Let's make this superior shift in realization. Let's elevate our awareness to a whole new level of genuine sincerity. Let's embrace the truth, by telling the truth.

VITALITY

"Ugh! Man, does my stomach ever hurt!" cried Boobee. "Maybe eating all those chips wasn't such a great idea."

Brrrrraaapp!

Boobee let out a tremendous burp, and I echoed with one of my own.

"Yeah, my gut is not feeling so good either," I said.

The two of us sat amidst the carnage of empty bags and cartons. Having just finished our first day of selling potato chips in the front foyer, we now sat in the concession stand stock room. We found ourselves surrounded by all our favorites. Boxes and bags of chips and other snacks. We're talking Munchos, Hickory Sticks, barbecue chips, sour cream and onion. We even had the biggest bags of Cheddacorn I'd ever seen. Plus a giant, stainless steel refrigerated chest chock full of all kinds of juice: orange, apple, grape, cranberry. Even grapefruit.

But best of all, the motherlode. Yes, the refrigerator contained the number one favorite beverage at our elementary school—chocolate milk!

Boobee and I had just demolished countless bags of crispy, salty potato goodness and washed them down with sweet slurps of the liquid chocolate gold. Bellies churning, we stared at the ridiculous mess littering the floor.

Arrrrgggghhh!

"I don't think Munchos and chocolate milk is a good combo," I moaned.

"You're not kidding," Boobee whimpered. "I feel like my tummy is going to explode!"

With a virtual all-you-can eat buffet of chips and sugary drinks at our disposal, we had thought we hit the jackpot. Knocking down as many goodies as possible, as fast as possible, seemed like the obvious challenge and opportunity. But in the throes of serious indigestion, we realized our dream come true had morphed into a nightmare.

Bleeeechhh!

"Do you think we should go see the nurse?" asked Boobee.

"No way, man. I already got heck from her earlier this week when I pretended to have a hernia."

"What's a hernia?" asked Boobee.

"I think it's when something pops out of your butt," I explained. Boobee laughed and then clutched his belly and moaned.

The discomfort only grew stronger. Gurgling and squirting digestive juices bubbled over in our bellies, like an evil potion in a witch's cauldron.

"What should we do?" Boobee asked. And then it hit me.

"I know! Let's go see Mr. Clifferd. Maybe he'll have some ideas."

We shuffled across the hallway to the boiler room. Most of the kid's in school would have knocked first, but we just walked right in like we owned the place. (We were down with Mr. Clifferd like that).

The warm air from the furnace enveloped us, welcoming us to the cozy confines of the space. The room was full of cleaning supplies, various mops, brooms, and a variety of tools. But rather than industrial cleaning chemicals, we could smell Mr. Clifferd's Aqua Velva cologne wafting in the balmy air.

In the far corner stood a small, rickety table with ringed coffee stains on its laminate surface. Mr. Clifferd sat in his usual spot doing his daily crossword puzzle.

He looked up from his paper with an inviting smile—not at all perturbed by our intrusion.

"Well, well, my young lads! What brings you in today?"

"We're not feeling so good, Mr. C.," answered Boobee. "I think my belly is about to burst!"

"Yeah, it's not looking too good for us," I added. "Maybe we have some kind of tropical disease. Like the bubonic plague or something?"

"They named a plague after me?" asked Boobee.

Mr. Clifferd laughed aloud.

"Don't worry, boys. I'm no medical doctor, but I can tell you this: you definitely *don't* have the bubonic plague."

"What the heck is going on with our guts, then?" I asked.

"Well, let's start with this. What did you guys have for lunch today?"

"Uh, well, today was our first day on chip duty," Boobee murmured. His chin fell to his chest.

"And?" Mr. Clifferd prompted.

"And…we kind of ate some of the inventory?" I half-asked, half-confessed.

"*Some* of the inventory?" Mr. Clifferd repeated. "How much did you two eat?"

"After the first few bags, I guess we lost count," Boobee admitted.

I chimed in: "We likely set a new school record. Let's just say it was somewhere between one and one hundred bags of chips."

Mr. Clifferd chuckled at my comment with loving concern on this face.

"Boys, I think you have your answer," he said.

"We do?" we asked in unison.

"Yes, my good men, we do. Your tummies are upset because of what you ate for lunch today. It's not just how *much* you put in your belly. It's also *what* you actually put in there. If you ask me, what we choose to put in our mouths is the biggest factor on our overall health."

"So, like Munchos, chocolate milk, Cheddacorn, Hickory Sticks...," began Boobee.

"Well, yes, those are the likely culprits for you both today. But it's not just snacks and junk food," said Mr. Clifferd.

"I'm talking about *everything* that goes in your mouth. Food, drinks, alcohol, cigarettes, or even medicine. The things we consume with our mouths enter our bodies. They go into the stomach and even into our bloodstream. And *that's* why I say what we put in our mouth has the largest single impact on our health."

"I thought going outdoors and getting exercise was the most important thing," I said.

"Well, that's definitely important, too, Chris. Getting outdoors, breathing in fresh air and moving your body is always a good idea," said Mr. Clifferd.

"What about stress, Mr. Clifferd?" asked Boobee. "I heard stress is a killer. And honestly, it seems like our teachers and parents freak out all the time over nothing!" Mr. Clifferd laughed.

"Yes, for sure, stress can play a huge role in your overall health," said Mr. Clifferd. "It all ultimately comes down to the simple choices we make. Do we nourish our one and only body with healthy food and cool, clean water? Choose to enjoy the fresh air of nature and get in some physical activity every day? Decide to go with the flow and not get worked up over the little things in life? It's these daily decisions that count more than we realize, my young friends."

"Thanks, Mr. Clifferd," said Boobee. "My belly feels better already!"

"Yeah, thanks, Mr. Clifferd. It all makes sense," I added.

"Anytime, laddies," said Mr. Clifferd with a wink and a smile. "Now, you should probably get back to the concession room and clean up the wreckage, so it's not left for the custodian to handle, right?"

We all laughed, and with a wave, Boobee and I headed out the door to tackle our cleanup job.

No one likes a tummy ache. We've all experienced the pain and suffering that comes with an upset stomach. Most of the time, it's our choices and behavior that lead to our discomfort.

As Mr. Clifferd taught us, what we decide to eat and drink, how we move our bodies, and our thoughts and beliefs all influence how we feel and our overall sense of wellness.

VITALITY

Everyone enjoys feeling great, filled with boundless energy and vitality. The secret to these experiences lies in our daily decisions.

The human body is an astounding creation. Meditate on the design and complexity of your body, and you'll find yourself in awe of its marvelous abilities. Our anatomies contain an elaborate arrangement of biological systems that enable us to perform a myriad of tasks, and allow us an incredible measure of sensory pleasures.

Our health colors our perception of the quality of our lives, and even our perception of the world itself. Just think about it, and you'll discover it for yourself. Imagine a sharp turn in your health—either a leapfrog improvement, or a drastic decline. Wouldn't a change like that alter how you viewed yourself and the world? Add a severe kink to your neck and see how that affects your attitude and excitement about the day. I don't mean to imply that our physicality alone determines our internal state. But we must admit it plays a significant role.

Let's honor the handiwork of the human form—our bodies. It's up to us to nourish, cherish, and respect our bodies. To fuel them with the right sustenance that will lead to optimal performance. The old saying holds true: *you are what you eat.*

The COVID-19 virus can strike anyone. If we want to contend with this aggressive invader, we would be wise to nurture our natural defenses.

Our immune systems remain on guard against whatever threats come our way. Doesn't it make sense to do as much as we can to boost our body's ability to defend us and keep us healthy?

Give your temple what it wants and needs, and let it take care of the rest. Our anatomy has its own intelligence and wisdom. It knows what to do, without us even being aware of it. Do you have to "will" your heart to beat? Your lungs to breathe? Your food to digest? Eyes to blink? Of course not. These are natural processes, guided by the intelligence baked into our bodies. We can provide the right conditions and environment for our bodies to prevail. You take care of your body, and your body will take care of you. It's a beautiful, symbiotic relationship.

If we follow Mr. Clifferd's advice and stick to the basics: plenty of fresh air, clean water, and nutritious food, along with some stress-releasing exercise and optimistic thinking, we can triumph over any challenges that come our way.

Keep it simple. Keep it consistent. And your body will reward you handsomely for the effort.

EARTH: OUR GLORIOUS COMMON HOME

"Check it out, man! This is incredible!" said Dooey.

"I know! I can't believe my eyes," I yelled back. "There must be a million of them up there!"

The two of us stared at the sky, astonished by what unfolded overhead. The armada of birds filled us with wonder.

"Thousands and thousands of them—and they all look the same!" Dooey said. "What kind are they?"

"I can't tell. But they're pretty big," I said.

"And they're all flying in the same direction. Where the heck are they going?".

"I have no idea," I answered. "You know what? They look like…Holy smokes, man…They're all blue jays!"

"No way. Seriously?" asked Dooey.

"Yeah, totally. You can tell by the color of their wings," I responded.

This was definitely a sight that we had never experienced before. We had both seen this beautiful blue and white bird before, but never more than one or two at a time. And now, a countless number of them flapped their wings and zoomed toward the lake in a breathtaking spectacle of nature.

It was early October in southern Ontario. We later learned the birds were migrating—heading south for the winter.

The blue jays seemed to come from out of nowhere, an endless stream.

"Wow, this is unreal!" said Dooey. "No one will believe us!"

"No kidding," I said. "They'll think we were hallucinating."

The only time we had ever seen anything similar was when we took a field trip to Point Pelee, to witness the monarch butterfly migration. The orange and black-winged beauties gather at the national park on their way south towards the fir trees of Mexico. They congregate by the thousands on the branches and leaves of the park's Carolinian forest before continuing onward for warmer weather.

"Hey, this reminds me of that time we saw those flying ants," said Dooey.

"Oh yeah," I remarked. "That was crazy!"

"For sure, those things were weird," Dooey replied. "Hey, remember when Alfie said some of them got in his pants, and he slid his bum all along the grass, trying to squish them?"

I laughed. "Only Alfie could have something like that happen. I think he even got some kind of rash down there."

As we giggled about Alfie's misfortune, the blue jays continued their overhead cruise. We stood in amazement, watching the colossal collection of birds seeking their southerly destination.

"I am never going to forget this, man," said Dooey.

"Me neither," I agreed. "I can't wait to tell Mr. Clifferd about this one. He's going to love it."

"Do you think he'll believe us?" Dooey asked.

"Of course. He always loves stories about nature, wildlife, and anything related to the great outdoors," I replied.

"I'm going to tell everybody at school tomorrow," Dooey said. "We are so lucky to have witnessed this."

"Yeah, I know. Sometimes you just have to keep your eyes peeled," I said.

Dooey agreed. "You just gotta pay attention, right?"

"Exactly," I answered. "Just think of all the people within a square mile who could watch this right now...if their eyes were open. Life is full of great surprises when we keep our eyes open. But most people miss these everyday miracles. Just think, it's possible we are the only two people on the planet seeing this!"

I'll never forget that day when Dooey and I beheld nature's grandeur. Wave after wave of thousands of beautiful blue jays. What a magical exhibition of the natural world's magnificence. I consider myself fortunate to glimpse that fantastic parade of colorful migrating birds.

The earth offers an inspiring abundance of astonishing diversity. The ecological splendor available to human beings staggers the imagination. Our planet provides a mind-blowing variety of environmental wonders. Appreciating our planet's riches can humble our hearts. The First Nations have always recognized a sacred reliance upon and connection with Mother Earth. They honor the natural systems that sustain us with clean air to breathe, crisp, clear water to drink, and nourishing, tasty food to eat. They aspire to revere the home that provides them with a bounty of stimulation and sustenance. Many of us in the modern, Western, colonized world are awakening to the Aboriginal wisdom of venerating our glorious planet. It's quite a prodigious dance they do with nature.

Have you ever heard of a man named Dr. David Suzuki? He's a Canadian scientist and environmental activist who has always been ahead of his time. Dr. Suzuki values this hallowed connection that humans have with the earth. His advocacy for nature spans many decades. Now in his eighties, his message of living in balance with the natural world is now being heard by humanity.

I'll bet if they had ever met, Dr. Suzuki and Mr. Clifferd would have been great friends. They both esteemed the majesty of nature. Maybe they could have gone camping together and enjoyed the wonders of the boreal forest or the deciduous woodlands. Wherever they may have ventured, I am confident they would have enjoyed each other's company and their shared love of the environment.

As I write these words, I'm gazing out our big bay window, noticing the signs of autumn's arrival. The changing colors of the trees. Crimson and gold leaves flutter in the wind. The sky grows a little greyer, and the air blowing in feels cool and smells crisp.

Seeing and sensing the unfolding changes invites me to introspection. Winter will be here before we know it—a season where everything slows down, especially here in Canada.

Isn't it amazing how much the weather can affect our moods? It reminds me of a theory I once heard. It suggests climate has a direct correlation with one's sense of humor.

Those who grow up in a cloudy, rainy place, like parts of England, project a more dark, sarcastic kind of humor. Those who live in a cold, snowy climate like portions of Russia often exhibit a sullen, stoic sort of levity. And those from hot, sunny spots like Jamaica likely prefer an easy-going, joyous type of amusement.

We sometimes lose sight of how much the elements surrounding us can affect us. Temperature, sunshine, and precipitation (or lack thereof) can influence our perception of life itself. Meteorology has a much larger impact on us than we sometimes realize. The weather *surrounding* us often affects the weather we carry *within* us. Are we carrying within the light of a bright sunny day with blue skies as far as the eye can see? Or are we carrying a damp and dismal drizzle? Or perhaps dark, heavy clouds accompanied by intermittent tumultuous thunderstorms?

As we move into fall here in the northern hemisphere, the evening news brings forth more evidence of the climate challenges our planet faces.

Wildfires rage in California. Hurricanes brew in the Caribbean. Floods devastate parts of Europe. Glacial ice falls into warming oceans.

Our earth is crying out and trying to tell us something. Are we listening? Do we hear the voice growing louder? Will we respond to these ubiquitous signs of unrest and agitation? When will we comprehend our vulnerability within this womb we inhabit?

Perhaps it's time for humanity to awaken to the cries arising from the natural world.

Perhaps the virus has come with an admonishing message for us: we've been ignoring our place as only a *part* of a much larger reality. We've been thinking it's all about *us*, neglecting both our fellow humans and the other creatures with whom we share this planet.

Perhaps we can recover our place in the grand scheme of life and appreciate how lucky we are to walk upon the soil of our glorious common home.

WISDOM

"Hey, quiet down over there!" she yelled. "Sit up straight! And don't you say another word…I'm warning you!"

Here we go again, I thought to myself. Another battle with my grade three teacher and arch-nemesis, Mrs. Focks.

This lady had it in for me. I mean, I was only in third grade—how bad could I have been? I swear, she lived to oppose everything that made it fun to be a kid.

"Wipe that smirk off your face, Buster, or you'll be sorry!" she shouted at me.

"What did I *do*?" I whined back in defiance.

"You know darn well what you did, Mr. Forman. You know the rules in this classroom!"

Ah, the rules.

Of course, it was always about the rules with this old battle-ax. I possessed a special talent of finding novel ways to violate her ever-expanding list of commandments.

"You do as I say, young man, or out you can go!" she threatened.

My frustration grew with every irritating word that spilled out of her mouth.

"Oh, you'd like that, wouldn't you?" I rifled back. "This isn't fair, you know!"

"I'll decide what's fair. That's how it works in here," she said with a growl.

Her beady eyes and annoying scowl made my blood boil. She wanted to break me, but I wouldn't let the bulldog prevail.

"Oh, really? So whatever you say goes?"

"Now, you're finally getting it, Mr. Forman," she sneered back, dripping with sarcasm.

We stared at each other with mutual disdain. I strained to avoid blinking or breaking eye contact. Instead, my gaze bore into her hideous face. I stood my ground. But the temptation was too great. I went for the jugular.

"Is it ever possible that you are wrong?"

"Maybe," she conceded. "But about this, I'm not!" she said. "Now, you sit there and keep your mouth shut. I don't want to hear another word out of you."

"But that's not…" I protested.

"That's it, Mister. You're done. Get out of here, right now!" she said, pointing to the doorway.

"But you can't…"

"OUT!"

She was now enraged, and my classmates sank down in their chairs to avoid attention. No one wanted to get caught in Mrs. Fock's crosshairs.

As for me, what could I do? I was on my own. I stood up and valiantly marched towards the door. Despite my show of confidence, dread washed over me.

I headed for the office, the place she had sent me so many times I lost count.

While I recognized I had been mouthy to Mrs. Focks, I also knew that her harsh, spirit-squashing command-and-control approach to the classroom wasn't right. We were just kids, after all. And somehow, someway, I had to take a stand. Just because she had the lion's share of the power didn't mean that she was always right. I'd have a fat chance of convincing the principal of that, though.

As I made my way to "the wall," I felt rage brewing inside me. My anger turned to total frustration and tears welled up in my eyes and a burning resentment filled my chest. I was so beside myself, I just wanted to scream and yell at the top of my lungs.

Why was she so nasty all the time? Why wouldn't she *ever* listen to *m*y side of the story? Why is life so hard sometimes?

As the tears rolled down my cheeks, I looked up, and there he was. Mr. Clifferd saw me crying. He approached me and knelt down to ask what was wrong. I could sense his sincere concern.

"You okay, my boy?" he asked.

"No, not really," I said, blubbering. "Mrs. Focks threw me out again. She's so mean."

"Really, is that so?" he asked. "What happened?" he asked with total interest.

"Does it even matter?" I sobbed. "I have to play by her rules, and believe me, Mr. C., most of the time they don't even make any sense."

"Is that right?" he asked with no judgment.

"Yeah, I swear, she does it on purpose. And I can't take it anymore. I'm never going back to her class again!"

"Hmm, I see. Well, what will you do then, my young friend?"

"I don't know. Maybe I'll…quit school and join the circus?" I had no qualifying skills, but it was the first answer that came to mind.

"Really? The circus…," he repeated with a chuckle. "Now that sounds interesting."

"Or…what if I went up north and became a lumberjack?" I thought maybe that sounded more realistic. Anyone can learn to swing an axe, right?

"Well…that is an option," he said with a smile.

"What am I supposed to do, Mr. Clifferd? She's so…so….unfair!"

"I know, I know," he said with understanding. "Life can be unfair."

"How come?" I asked with reeling grade three existential concern.

"It's like this, my boy," he began. "Sometimes people make up rules without considering the effect those rules might have on others."

"Yeah, why?" I asked.

"Well, probably because they haven't taken the time to understand what it's like to walk in another person's shoes," he said.

"What do you mean?" I said with a confused look on my face.

"That's a way of saying they didn't bother to understand what someone else is feeling, to see it from another's perspective," he explained.

"Why don't people do that?" I asked.

"There could be many reasons, my boy. I think most of the time, people aren't even aware of their choices," he responded. "Sometimes people don't even realize what they're doing. They act without thinking."

"You're not kidding!" I said.

Mr. Clifferd laughed. "It's alright, though, because you can always take the high road in these kinds of situations."

"The high road?" I had never heard that expression before, either.

"It's another metaphor. Like walking in someone else's shoes. Taking the high road means deciding to be kind and patient, even when you have every reason not to. It's choosing a nobler, wiser way to respond."

"How do you do that?" I asked.

"You start by trying your very best to figure out how the other person might see the situation," he replied. "Once you can see it from their perspective, it helps you understand their actions a bit more. You still might not like their actions or agree with them. But getting some insight into what they're thinking can help you calm down."

"You mean like trying to figure out why they do what they do?" I asked.

"Exactly, my boy!" he said. "The more you can do this, the easier life will be for you."

"Okay, Mr. C. I'll do my best to figure out what other people are feeling."

"Even Mrs. Focks?" he challenged.

"Ugh…" I began. It was easier to talk in theory, but when he mentioned her name, the emotions stirred up again. But I took a deep breath.

"Yeah, I guess so. I mean, I'll try," I began weakly. "For you, Mr. C., I'll really try."

"Good to hear, my boy. I know you can do it. Now, with that in mind, why do you think Mrs. Focks sent you to the office?"

I thought for a moment.

"Because she hates me," I said. Mr. Clifferd laughed again.

"No, no, Chris. You may not be her favorite student, but I don't think she *hates* you. Think about it for a moment."

"Well, I feel like she's always trying to take away our fun. And when she does, she gets really mean about it. And that makes me mad because I feel like it's really unfair."

"Why do you think she might want to 'take away your fun,' as you say?"

I thought for a few moments before responding.

"Well, last Friday, she was out sick. We had a substitute teacher. No one listened to the teacher. We all just fooled around the entire time, trying to see what we could get away with."

"I see," said Mr. Clifferd. "Was that fun?" he asked.

"Well, I mean, at the time, it was pretty funny," I said, a little embarrassed.

"I'll bet no one in the class learned anything that day, did they?"

"Not really," I admitted. I was starting to see his point.

"So, just imagine if Mrs. Focks ran the classroom like that every day," he said. "Would the students learn what they need to learn in the third grade?"

Mr. Clifferd then invited me to think about the concept of taking the high road and what it might look like if I took the high road with Mrs. Focks. He said he wasn't even asking me to do anything different. He just wanted me to *think* about it for now. *Really* think about it.

Mr. Clifferd was right, of course. (Like usual). If we desire to connect with others and attain a peaceful, loving harmony with our human family, we need to do our utmost to understand how others feel and to comprehend the experiences that may have led to their emotional state.

You've most likely heard of the Golden Rule. It's typically expressed as something like, "do unto others as you would have them do unto you." That's a good start. But I want to take this thoughtful suggestion to an even higher level. What if we turned this resolution into, "*Be* unto others as you would have them *Be* unto you."

You might think, *I don't get it, Chris. You just changed one word: be instead of do. So what?* Yes, it is just one word. The reason I propose this switch is that I believe practicing it this way brings us to a deeper, more powerful place. When we simply *do* something, it's just an action. It says nothing about the motivation or intention, or the way we are going about it. It says nothing about *who we are being* when we act. And that's the important distinction. When you *embody* your intentions and desires—when you go beyond *doing* them, and you *be* them—it amplifies your strength and impact.

When you *become your aspirations*, you will radiate a potent vibration. When you choose to embody your wishes, you will bring their potential, and your potential, to greater heights.

Do you want others to show courage in their lives?

> *Then start by BEING courageous yourself.*

Do you wish to witness more hope in the world?

> *Then choose to BE hope for others.*

Do you thirst for happiness and joy for all people?

> *Then BE joy, BE happiness to all you encounter, start with those with whom you live and interact each day.*

Finally, if you desire an awakening on the planet, then you know what to do…

> *BE awakening.*

It's about intention. But it's not about trying harder. Or even "trying" at all. It's about "being." In the words of one exalted sage, Master Yoda, "Do, or do not. There is no try." You are either going to *be* a certain way, or you are not.

When you are *being*, you embody what you intend. You exude it. Not only do you impart what you *be* to others, you impart it to yourself. It's a virtuous cycle.

This is the way of life. This is how loving energy moves.

Sometimes, when I am bartending, I will ask a guest how they're doing. In these challenging times of the pandemic, I hear responses like, "Well, Chris, I'm surviving."

Never mind their words, between the fatigued look on their face and the slump in their shoulders, I can sense their distress and weariness. In moments like these, I do my best to help the guest view their life from a fresh vantage point. I'll come back with an optimistic invitation to alter their perspective. I offer an opportunity to see that instead of just *surviving*, maybe they could be *thriving*! Or, better yet, *be* thriving.

Although times are tough right now, we can take pride in our ability to rise to the occasion. Maybe instead of feeling distraught and discouraged, we can appreciate how well we're contending with it all. Just think of the lessons we are learning on this bumpy ride and how those lessons can serve us in the future. We will be people who have survived a global pandemic. That's right—we are survivors! When we appreciate how living through difficulties strengthens us, it can change our entire perspective on what matters.

Have you ever felt envious? Do you sometimes long for someone else's life? Or the image they convey?

Have you said to yourself, "Damn, I wish that was me"?

If you have had these thoughts, it's okay. It sounds counterintuitive, but envy can serve as a positive motivator. The desire, the urge within, is trying to tell you something. It's letting you know you've come across something you find valuable—something you desire.

There's nothing wrong with feeling attracted to certain qualities or experiences. The key is in remaining aware of the motives behind your ambitions. Are they self-serving? Or do they call you to go outside yourself and contribute to others?

As human beings, we are always changing, whether or not we realize it. Nothing in this world stays the same. Impermanence is the reality we inhabit. It doesn't matter how much we try to resist the inevitable variations of being human. Change is happening—to our bodies, our minds, and our planet. It's natural for this to occur.

This continuous meandering and unfoldment keeps the ride of life interesting, exciting, and surprising. Most of us wouldn't have it any other way. We homo sapiens like our mystery. We enjoy a good drama. (Maybe that's why some of us create drama out of nothing!)

Sometimes we lose sight of our role in this exceptional theatrical extravaganza. When we realize our part in this amazing story, things get intriguing.

What if...our participation in this marvelous adventure matters?

What if...the person we choose to become can make a difference?

What if...we try to walk a mile in another person's shoes and feel what it's like to travel along their pathway?

What if...this is why we are all here in the first place?

You may have noticed the title of this chapter is Wisdom. Yet, I haven't used the word once yet. Why is that? Well, for one, wisdom is a journey rather than a destination. It's a path, a pursuit. If we think we have it, we certainly don't. Second, the primary tools for cultivating wisdom are questions. Questions lead us to answers—to deeper understanding.

Just asking a question is the first step. It demonstrates our openness to learning something new, to receiving an answer. Pursuing answers—tracking them down, trying them on, and testing them out—allows us to examine things from various angles and perspectives. To see the matter from another perspective.

Just like Mr. Clifferd encouraged me to do.

He was wise like that.

SANCTITY

*B**ang! Bang! Bang!*
The unmistakable sound of firecrackers rang out in the distance.
Pow! Pow! Pow!
"What the heck is that?" yelled Jonny.
Bang! Bang! Bang!
Pow! Pow! Pow!
Bang! Pow! Bang!
"What's going on back there?"
My heart sank as I heard the noise of the mini-explosions coming from the back of the schoolyard.
Pow! Pow! Bang!
"Seriously, what are those guys doing back there, man?" Jonny demanded.
"You don't want to know," I said, my eyes downcast.

"What do you mean?" Jonny asked, looking bewildered.

I couldn't bear to tell him. A nature lover, I could only imagine Jonny's distress if he discovered the senseless carnage taking place. My somber expression only fed his curiosity and persistence.

"C'mon, man. You have to know what's going on! Why won't you answer me?" he pleaded, just before another round began.

Pow! Bang! Bang! Pow!

"Fine, I'll find out myself!" said Jonny before taking off on foot. He headed toward the source of the noise, the marshy pond in the back.

"Hey, wait for me!" I called to no avail. I jumped up and broke into a sprint, attempting to catch up with my bud.

Jonny was a fast runner, especially when motivated by something exciting or urgent. I did my best to reach him as quickly as possible, concerned about his reaction when he made the sickening discovery.

The back of our school's property contained a small sanctuary of natural habitat. A green corridor ran parallel to the soccer field, just south of a set of train tracks. The stretch of land grew wild. Various native plants, trees, and insects populated the land. We often found praying mantises, grasshoppers, and even "walking stick" bugs. A grove of sumac trees and large poplars stretched into the sky. We spotted groundhogs, cottontail rabbits, and other small animals that lived in the lush shrubbery, along with butterflies, chicory, and milkweed.

My favorite feature of this beautiful oasis was a small pond, brimming with an incredible array of natural wonders. It was like a small piece of marshland had dropped from the sky and landed at the very back of our schoolyard.

This little pool of water teemed with life. Our science teacher once marched us out there, a mini-field trip to our native teaching exhibit on the outdoors. The pond featured cattails, lily pads, and duckweed. Dragonflies, blue herons, and red-winged blackbirds flew overhead, and turtles sometimes stretched their necks above the murky water's surface.

What stands out to me most of all are the frogs. If quantity proves dominance, they ruled the place. Starting in early spring each year, they'd strike up the orchestra, filling the area with their melodious chanting. With their shiny green skin and necks puffing out like a kid blowing bubble gum, watching and listening to the frogs always filled my heart with curiosity and amazement.

Jonny's too. And that's why I feared his devastation and heartbreak when he discovered the fate of these glorious treasures.

Jonny reached the pond a good thirty-seconds before me. I joined him to discover a scene even more gruesome than I'd feared. Jonny stood there with tears in his eyes as he looked at the carnage atop the bloody waters of the pond.

Several frogs floated on the surface. Some floated upon their backs. All of them lifeless and mangled, blown apart. Legs and arms torn off from the force of the explosions.

Disgusted and repulsed, a question arose from deep within.

Why?

Why would anyone want to do this?

Why would someone be so cruel and thoughtless?

A taunting voice severed my reverie.

"Awww, what's the matter, crybabies? Are your little feelings hurt?" asked Toby.

The main perpetrator spoke while his two henchmen snickered along.

"Are the little babies sad about the little froggies?" he continued.

A look of rage flashed across Jonny's face.

"How could you guys do this?" Jonny yelled.

"Do what?" Toby shot back. "Blow up some stupid, ugly toads. Who cares?"

"I care!" Jonny answered. "I can't believe you're so heartless!"

"Don't be such a goody two-shoes," said Toby. "It's fun to watch their heads explode. You should try it sometime."

"Fun? You call this fun?" Jonny said. "You're demented, Toby!"

"Oh yeah, what's that supposed to mean?"

"It means you're an idiot!"

"You better watch it, loser, or I'll pound you into the ground!"

Toby's faced turned red. He made a fist and stormed towards Jonny. No one ever messed with Toby. He was a big dude and known for his quick temper.

My stomach tightened. I feared the frogs might not be the only victims today. A stern voice called out from behind us.

"That's enough, boys! The show's over!"

It was Mr. Clifferd, in the nick of time—just before things got even messier.

"Toby, you get down to the office *right now*!" I'd never heard Mr. Cifferd raise his voice before.

"What for? I didn't do anything!"

"Now!" commanded Mr. C. Toby started moving.

As Toby walked toward the school, tears began streaming down Jonny's face. He sobbed involuntarily, and Mr. Clifferd put his arm on Jonny's shoulder.

"It's okay, son, just let it out," said Mr. C.

As Jonny continued to weep, I noticed Toby's cronies had slinked away. Meanwhile, a few other students arrived who had followed the noise. Some of those kids had tears in their eyes, too, moved by Jonny's open display of emotion and Mr. C's tenderness. And, of course, the vain and senseless loss of amphibian life grieved their hearts.

"How could they do this, Mr. Clifferd?" asked Jonny.

"My young friend, some people don't respect the sanctity of life," Mr. Clifferd began.

"But why would someone do such an awful thing?" asked Jonny.

"Often, people who do horrible things like this are missing something in their lives," Mr. Clifferd replied.

"Like what?"

"It's hard to say. Sometimes people crave attention, and they'll do anything for it. Maybe he doesn't feel loved and just wants someone to pay attention to him—even if it's negative attention."

"Hmm, it's hard to think of Toby as wanting love. He's always so mean to everyone. He doesn't seem to care about love at all."

"Whatever is going on with that boy, he must be feeling emotions he does not know how to handle."

"That's for sure," said Jonny. "I just don't see why he took it out on innocent creatures."

"I don't either, Jonny. I wish everyone recognized that life is sacred and deserves to be treated with love and respect."

"What about the gross, weird stuff, though?" I asked.

"You bet. Snakes, spiders. All of it, my boy. Humans are part of a much bigger reality. We're one piece of a magnificent puzzle. A thread in a beautiful tapestry. We're recent players on the scene, in a story that's been unfolding for millennia."

"What do you mean?" asked Jonny.

"Well, think about it. Dinosaurs roamed the earth millions of years ago before they became extinct. Do you know what other creature was alive back then that's still alive now?"

"Umm, weren't there cavemen back then?" asked Jonny. Mr. Clifferd laughed.

"No, not quite, Jonny. Cavemen came a long time after the dinosaurs. But you are close—the creatures I'm thinking of did live in caves at the time of the dinosaurs."

"I know—bats!" I said.

"Good guess, Chris. But that's not it, either. Believe it or not, cockroaches crawled around caves at the time of the dinosaurs. And amazingly, cockroaches survived whatever wiped out the dinosaurs."

"No way! Cockroaches?" said Jonny.

"That's right, my boy. It's humbling to think that the lowly cockroach has been hanging out on planet earth for millions of years longer than humans. And they are *still* here. If cockroaches survived the dinosaurs, who knows, maybe they'll be here long after humans, too?"

"Wow, so even cockroaches are special," I said.

"Like I said, all life is sacred," said Mr. Clifferd. "Like I said, though, not *everyone* believes that. And

I'm afraid if we don't get ourselves back inside fast, Mr. Hikkling might wipe *us* off the face of the planet!" Mr. Clifferd. We all laughed together and headed toward the school.

"I'll tell you one thing," said Jonny. "I'll never look at a cockroach the same way after today!"

"And I don't think I'll ever *squish* a cockroach again!" I added.

I'll never understand what motivated Toby and his buddies to massacre frogs with firecrackers. You might shake your head and think, *Ack, he was just a kid.* And you'd have a point. Yet, I often scratch my head at the behavior of many adults today. Some people can be so insensitive and careless, and it breaks my adult heart, just as it broke my grade school heart.

Just the other day, I watched a car pull out of a fast-food restaurant parking lot. The driver tossed a bag out the window, right into the street. (When I see trash around the city, I used to think, *Who are the people who do this?* Now I know. Well, one of them, at least)

A paper bag on the street may not seem as extreme as stuffing live firecrackers into the orifices of frogs (and certainly not as violent). But it still betrays a sad disregard for our planet, and I'd argue it is a type of violence.

Human history offers disturbing examples of atrocities committed against mankind, and outrageous actions inflicted upon the natural world. Blood stains our hands. Our collective disdain for sentient life is reprehensible. Utter disrespect for creation has frayed the interwoven fabric—the tapestry Mr. Clifferd spoke of—binding all of life together.

Our malicious actions have resulted in the slaughter of countless living creatures of all kinds. We're often oblivious to the suffering and destruction of our world's astounding biodiversity. Tropical rainforests occupy less than seven percent of the earth's land. These forests represent the "lungs of the planet," as they generate roughly twenty percent of the world's oxygen. Yet, everyone reading these words has heard of the ravages of deforestation.

We've seen massive migrations of people trying to escape wanton decimation of both humanity and its natural home. It's time to open our eyes to the blatant contempt we've shown to both our human family, and to the incredible planet that sustains us.

What better choices can we make as a unified family to ensure our decisions come from a higher, more evolved consciousness? Such positive choices will require acknowledging that all life deserves veneration. Mindless killing and eradication must stop. To advance as a species, we must cease our butchering of everything sacrosanct in this world.

Let's shed primitive ways of dealing with conflict and discord. Our archaic approach to settling our differences does not work.

Our collective consciousness cries out for an absolute and decisive choice to end the bloodshed.

Will we answer the call before it's too late?

COOPERATION

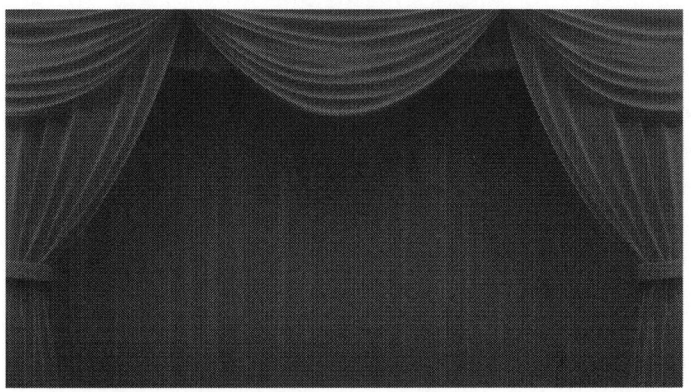

"Pssst! Forman, they're looking for you!" whispered my friend Jeff. "Hurry. You can hide behind this curtain."

I slipped backstage, my heart pounding. Any sound or sudden movement, and I would blow my cover.

How did I get myself into this situation?

The play had been a bit boring for my taste. I squirmed in my seat through half the show, wishing I was hanging with my buddies who were helping backstage. I took some action to make that happen, and the next thing I knew, a pack of teachers were hunting me down like I'd robbed a bank or something.

"Alright, Jef, where is he?" asked Mrs. Koz. "We know he's back here, somewhere."

"Gee, I don't know," replied Jef with a faux authenticity that could have qualified him for a role on the other side of the curtain.

"Maybe you should check on the other side?" offered Jef.

"We already checked that side. I know he's around here, mister, and you're going to tell me where."

Mrs. Koz glowered at Jef, a stern look on her wrinkled face. That intimidating stare had scared many a student into submission.

"Did you check the supply room?" asked Jef.

"If I find out you're hiding him from us, you're in big trouble."

Mrs. Koz snarled as she turned and slinked down the stairs and around the corner, headed for the school's supply room.

"Whoa man, that was a close one," said Jef. "She's out to get you."

"Tell me about it. How will I get myself out of this pickle?" I asked.

We were standing in the back corner of the school's gymnasium, tucked away behind a huge velvet curtain. To our left was the rear exit to a short passageway that ran directly behind the school's performing arts stage. On the other side of the curtain, just a few feet away, we could hear our thespian classmates performing with great emotion. In this part of the play, the characters engaged in an escalating argument. I knew the noisy exchange would only last a couple of minutes. If I acted fast, maybe I could find a new hiding place during the commotion on stage.

"Duck down the passageway and hide on the other side," Jef suggested.

"No way, man. Mr. McLeen and Ms. Steel are over there. I'll get busted for sure."

"Well, you can't stay here. Mrs. Koz is already suspicious of me."

With limited options for escape, I felt the pressure mount as each second ticked by.

I couldn't take the back hallway behind the stage—they'd catch me if I went that route.

I couldn't take the side staircase where Mrs. Koz had just gone—that would bring me right out in the open in front of the entire audience. Utter doom and complete humiliation.

There was a metal ladder on the wall just above our heads—but no one had ever dared to climb it and go through the secret hatch for fear of setting off the fire alarm.

My buddy Nak emerged from the back hallway, and when he spotted me, a concerned look spread across his face.

"Whoa, man...you are in for it!" said Nak.

"I know. You have any ideas?" I asked him.

"Wait!" said Jef. "There is one possibility. But... it's pretty crazy," said Jef.

I looked at him.

"You could hide under the bed," said Jef.

"The bed?" asked Nak. "You mean the one on the stage?"

"Bingo."

"Are you crazy, man? The audience will see me."

"Not necessarily. There's a skirt around the bottom of the bed."

"You want me to crawl under the bed that's on the stage right in the middle of the play?"

"Got any better ideas?" asked Jef.

"Not really. But how would I even get under it without being spotted?"

"I know," said Nak. "Adrian showed me a small opening that goes from the back hallway to right behind the rear of the stage. You could squeeze through it and dive under the bed."

"That could work," said Jef.

"Easy for you to say, Jef. It's not your big butt that's sliding through the hole. But I guess that's my best option at this point."

Nak jumped in with a suggestion.

"I'll go back down the passageway and have Adrian distract the teachers. When you see me give the thumbs up, head for the opening."

I could feel the butterflies in my stomach as I contemplated this mad dash for safety. A bead of sweat rolled down my temple. If I could reach the hole in time and wiggle through, I'd still need to shimmy under the bed without drawing attention.

Of course, this predicament was my own doing.

If I had just stayed in my seat like the other students in the audience, I'd be fine right now. Actually, that's not true. I'd be bored beyond belief. That's why I snuck backstage. Ugh, I should have played sick today. I could be home watching The Love Boat *right now.*

"You doing this, or what?" asked Nak.

I gave him a nod. He whisked back down the passageway to enroll Adrian in our plan. *Would she cooperate with our plan?* I needed her to divert my would-be captors. My plan wouldn't work without her help. My fate now laid in Adrian's hands.

I stuck my head around the corner. Peering down the hallway, I spotted Nak talking to someone just out of my line of vision. He was looking up at whomever he was speaking with, so I could tell it must be the teachers. After a couple of torturous minutes, Nak turned in my direction and gave a thumbs up.

It was now or never. I sprinted down the passage towards the rumored opening, praying it was there. I scurried along the narrow corridor, my eyes focused on finding that space in the wall—my ticket to the undercover hideaway.

Nak pointed to a spot on the right wall with a small wooden knob sticking out. I slid to a dead stop, then grabbed the knob. A two-foot door swung open. There was a cavity in the wall, just like Nak said. I dove headfirst into the opening, smacking my head on the way in. I squirmed all the way through and shut the hatch behind me. My chest heaved as I gasped for air. My ears rang from the self-inflicted blow to my head. A trickle of blood slid down my temple. There was no time to worry about a bonk to the old noodle. I had to find that bed.

My eyes assessed the terrain. I was now directly behind the stage. Before me sat a large piece of plywood covered with a black cloth. It served as a backdrop for the performance. The backdrop was the only thing between the two-hundred odd people in the audience, and me. I spotted my refuge—the glorious bed. The guys were right. It had a skirt around it. Except the skirt didn't reach the floor. A clear gap sat between the red and black checkered fabric and the wooden surface of the stage.

Even though the opening was just a few inches away, I trembled at the thought of sliding under the frame of the bed and getting busted by a sharp eye in the crowd. As I pondered my circumstances, Adrian came into view. She motioned with urgent vigor, directing me to get under the bed. Perhaps the teachers were closing in. Maybe this was my last chance.

The audience broke into applause, and the main curtain closed, signaling a major scene had just finished. The stage crew rushed to reset the stage, arranging sets and props for the next scene. *This is my chance*, I thought. With all my might, I propelled my body towards the underside of the bed. I did it! I had positioned myself on my belly, under the bed, and held my breath, trying to not make a single sound.

Would this new hiding place provide my much-needed protection? Or would my pursuers find me and drag me out by my feet before thrashing me with a cat-o-nine-tails?

I appealed to a higher power.

Oh please, please, please don't let me get caught in this ridiculous position!

Lying motionless on my stomach, I heard the voices of the night stalking teachers getting closer. Or was it my imagination? No, it was Mrs. Koz.

"He's gotta be here, somewhere. I'm going to catch that little bugger if it's the last thing I do!"

"We've searched everywhere. Maybe he snuck out somehow?" said Mr. McLeen.

"Yeah, he must have gotten away," said Ms. Steel.

"I'm going to find that little demon," said Mrs. Koz.

"Suit yourself," replied Mr. McLeen. "But I'm going to enjoy the rest of the show."

"Yeah, me, too." said Ms. Steel. "I've had enough of this wild goose chase."

"Keep looking if you wish, but I'm heading back now," said Mr. McLeen.

"That makes two of us," replied Ms. Steel.

I then heard footsteps moving away, and the volume of their voices diminished as they faded into the distance.

Holy moly, I thought to myself. *I made it! I made it!*

Talk about a sigh of relief. My heart had been pounding so fast, I thought my chest was going to explode. I could now take a breath, and avert a mini heart attack. I still wasn't out of the woods, though. I still had to hope that when the main curtain reopened for the next scene no one in the crowd would spot the boy laying commando-style under the central prop.

I closed my eyes, crossed my fingers, and said another prayer as I awaited my fate. Before I knew it, the velvet curtain slid again across the surface of the pine floor. I squeezed my eyelids even tighter, willing myself to not move a single, solitary cell of my body. The slightest involuntary twitch could spell certain disaster.

The piano played, and the lead actor broke into song. I once again held my breath. I could almost see the headline in the paper.

Extra! Extra! Read All About It!

Curly-Haired Kid Caught Lying Under Bed on Stage in School Play

Every second felt like torture. *Would someone spot me? Would a concerned parent yell out, "Hey, there's someone hiding under the bed." After a flawlessly-executed escape, would Mrs. Koz get her hungry hands of justice on me?*

The music and singing carried on, and as the ballad reached its crescendo, I opened my eyes again. Blinking a few times, my vision cleared, and I found myself looking upon the audience, gazing just above their heads. The stage lights were bright, and the feet of my theatrical classmates danced across the stage as the song reached a climactic finish. The crowd burst into applause as the players shuffled into position for the next scene.

A guardian angel must have been looking out for me that day because I never got caught. I thanked my lucky stars for avoiding a spectacle that would have cost my future self countless hours of expensive therapy. While I may have patted myself on the back for pulling off the stunt, I could never have pulled it off alone. Without the help of my trusty classmates, I'd still be serving detention for Mrs. Koz today.

My friends and I worked together to make my daring evasion a success.

Call it teamwork.

A joint effort.

An alliance.

Call it whatever you like.

All I know is that it worked, and it wouldn't have happened without cooperation.

The victory that day reminded me of those Olympic relay races where runners pass a baton to a teammate to run the next leg of the race. Each member of the relay team needs to count on themselves, and the other members, to give their very best effort to ensure a favorable outcome. Just as we won't win a relay race without a strong alliance, we won't change the world without a harmonious, concerted effort.

We must choose the path of collaboration and unity to deal with the coronavirus and reach new heights as a human family.

Have you ever seen an Amish barn-raising or watched the Jehovah's Witnesses build a kingdom hall? I've witnessed these events, and they are beautiful sights that display mutual respect and connection. Everyone plays a role in helping to create a structure that they can embrace. Whether it's putting up the walls, securing the roof, or making sure everyone gets a cold drink and something good to eat, everyone works together in a grand display of communion. Everyone involved in the effort will benefit from the end product.

In elementary school, gym class offered students an opportunity to add physical activity into the day.

COOPERATION

One of my favorite gym class activities involved a parachute. We would gather outside in the grassy field. With the parachute laying on the grass, we'd stand around and encircle it. The gym teacher then instructed us to reach down, and pick up the edge of the parachute, and in unison, lift the parachute.

Thanks to laws of physics that I can't explain, the parachute would fill with air and billow. We'd raise and lower the parachute several times, building energy and momentum. Once we got it going, if we hung on tight, the rising parachute would lift us off our feet and into the air. The momentary weightlessness felt like magic. I felt like a bird taking flight, even if only for a few seconds and a few inches.

The parachute game does not work the same with a single player. Oh sure, if the parachute is light enough, you might get some air under it. But to get it to lift you off the ground requires other players. When a group of players works together to harness the forces of nature, it creates magic. The impossible becomes possible. It's a glorious feeling, taking part in the collective effort, cooperating with the laws of nature and physics, and rising to new heights. As I write these words, I can still feel that gravity-defying force lifting me off the ground with a gentle tug.

As we move into the second wave of the pandemic, the emotional and financial strain mounts as the weeks go by. As pressure increases, families, individuals, businesses, and other organizations search for the best ways to cope with this new reality.

Some families have combined households. We see adults moving back in with their older parents. Elderly grandmas deciding to live with a grandchild. Families inviting parents or in-laws to stay with them. Siblings and cousins opting to share an apartment. Whatever the arrangements, the changed circumstances brought on by COVID-19 have pushed folks into arrangements they may not have otherwise considered.

These various arrangements remind me of older, traditional, and aboriginal ways of familial living, with multi-generations living under one roof. Perhaps it's a positive development. We're recovering and rediscovering family solidarity. Families looking after each other and sharing responsibilities may foster a wider community solidarity.

It's always beneficial when individuals combine effort for a common cause, aligning their energy on a shared prosperity and happiness for everyone involved. Re-embracing the unifying power and wisdom of the family could help evolve our species, opening new realms of possibility and achievement. We will never have love, peace, and cooperation in the wider human family until we see it under the roofs of individual families.

When we learn to value cooperation at home, and witness first-hand how it enriches everyone, we will glimpse a cooperative community. Empowered by this vision, we can spread it to our neighborhoods, our cities, our countries, and the world.

INTEGRITY

"Go...go...go...c'mon...that's it...faster...yeah...now we're moving!" I cried out. "Ok...here comes the corner...we'll take it wide this time!"

The metal wheels of the rickety wooden cart clicked across the slick linoleum floor.

Clickety clack...clickety clack...

The faster Crowse ran, the louder the noise of the wheels echoed throughout the hallway.

"Nice man...that was a sweet turn!" I called out. "Alright...let's hit this next part at warp speed!"

Crowse charged down the hallway, pulling the rope with all his might.

Clickety clack...clickety clack...clickety clack...

"Go...go....yeah...yeah...we're gonna set a new track record! Gangway...coming through!"

I could feel the vibrations from the wheels tickling my legs as we ripped along towards the school's library. Since there were no handles, I had to grip onto the sides of the clapboard wagon. We were attempting to hit maximum velocity and reach a pace that no other kid had ever attained.

The wagon's usual purpose involved delivering little cartons of milk to each classroom. Oh, we had the milk on board, alright; a fine selection of both white and chocolate. But the delivery would have to wait. We had a larger goal to accomplish. We were talking *warp speed*, after all.

Clickety clack...clickety clack...

"Ok...now pull a 180 and get ready!" I hollered. "It's time to burn rubber!"

Crowse huffed and puffed as he yanked the rope. The wagon spun around, and we prepared for an unprecedented rate of acceleration—one the halls of our school had never witnessed.

"We're about to go down in history as the fastest of all time!".

"Are you sure about this?" Crowse asked.

"Definitely!"

"But what about the planters at the end of the hallway?"

"No problemo! This thing corners like a dream... we'll whip right past them."

"What about Ms. Schmitts? If she catches us, we're toast!"

"Don't worry about her. She'll never even know what happened."

"I don't know about this, Chris..." began Crowse.

"C'mon, man...we can tell everyone at lunchtime how we set a new land speed record! Including Keri."

Crowse had a crush on Keri. Big time. He got shaken and stirred whenever she walked by. Maybe the idea of impressing her would generate some extra horsepower?

"You think she'd be impressed?"

"No question. This is warp speed. Maybe she'll even give you a kiss."

"Maybe you're right. What girl wouldn't be excited about warp speed?"

Crowse pulled the rope taut, and I leaned forward, assuming racing position. With no steering wheel, I had to balance my weight just right, like a toboggan on wheels. No steering wheel, no brakes, no control. Just a whole bunch of crazy.

We picked up speed. Crowse broke into a measured gallop, saving some energy for the second half of the hallway. That's where we would really hit our stride.

Clickety clack...clickety clack...clickety clack...

The squeaky wheels turned with increasing intensity as we sped down the track.

"Go man...yeah...now you're hitting it...go...go...go!"

The milk cart moved faster and faster as we barreled down the corridor towards the office all the way at the end of the hallway. Two large pots filled with tropical plants sat just outside of Ms. Schmitts' door. The cart zoomed forward.

Clickety clack...clickety clack...

We crossed the mid-point of the hallway, and the pitch of the screeching wheels raised up an octave.

"This is it, Crowse...maximum power, baby!"

Clickety clack...clickety clack...

We were flying.

"Get ready for the corner, Chris. Here it comes!"

We had taken this turn many times, but never at this velocity. As the cart propelled toward the office, I realized no amount of body weight shifting would allow the cart to execute the ninety-degrees necessary to cruise past the office and continue down the hall. I clutched the edge of the wagon, reckoning with the truth: we had lost all control over the wooden milk wagon.

I shouted for Crowse to put on the brakes, but it was far too late. I shut my eyes, grabbed the rope, and prepared for impact.

KABOOM!!!

The cart smashed into the planters outside the office. I went airborne along with a mix of leaves, dirt, and chocolate milk. What goes up must come down, and a moment later, I found myself covered in a mess of dirt, leafy vines, and milk.

"Holy crow! Are you alright?" Crowse asked in disbelief.

I surveyed my body for signs of broken bones or gushing blood. Other than a deep throbbing in one leg and gritty mud on my face, I seemed unscathed. Milk drenched my pants, and I spotted one of my shoes sitting by a piece of the decimated planter just outside of Ms. Schmitts' office.

"We are dead ducks, man," said Crowse.

With my head still spinning, a familiar and formidable screech assaulted my senses.

"Mr. Forman! What the heck have you done now?"

It was Ms. Schmitts. I didn't even have to look up to know that voice. I could feel the heat from the fire and brimstone flowing out of her nostrils. Her petite size did little to diminish our fears. A dragon is a dragon, no matter how small.

"Out with it, young man! I can't wait to hear this one."

Still stunned from the disastrous crash, I had enough wits about me to stay calm and measured. But the right words eluded me still.

"Well…you see…it's kind of like…well, you see…it just sort of happened."

"Just…sort of…happened?" Ms. Schmitts repeated in a mocking whisper. "How on God's green earth does a ridiculous mess like this JUST SORT OF HAPPEN?"

"I sort of lost control…".

"We deliver milk to every classroom, every day, and no one has ever lost control. How could you possibly lose control?" she asked, gesturing toward the demolished wagon sitting upside down.

"It's like it has a mind of its own. It does whatever it wants."

"Do you honestly expect me to believe that?"

She turned her attention to my partner in crime.

"And what about you, Mr. Crowse? What do you have to say about all this?"

Crowse stood there, bewildered and speechless.

"Well, mister?"

"The classrooms needed their milk…?" Crowse began weakly.

I couldn't take it anymore. It had been my idea all along, and I couldn't let Crowse take the fall.

"It wasn't his fault, Ms. Schmitts!" I blurted out. "He was just pulling the rope."

"And?"

"The cart started going berserko!" I answered.

"Yeah, it just went crazy," Crowse added, finding some confidence.

"So you two expect me to believe that the milk cart did this damage all by itself?"

"Well, not exactly," I offered. "Just right at the end."

"At the end of what?"

INTEGRITY

"Have you ever heard of warp speed?" I asked.

We could see the steam coming out of her ears. Usually, in these circumstances, the offenders would either make up a ludicrous lie and dig an even deeper hole, or they would crack under Ms. Schmitt's interrogation, and burst into tears.

Crowse and I had neither lied nor conceded guilt. We told it like it was, as we saw it.

We never intended on harming the wagon, the milk, or Ms. Schmitts' beloved tropical plants. We were simply striving to set an imaginary school record. We held our integrity to the bitter end and felt proud about standing in our truth.

Ms. Schmitts ordered us to report to the janitor's room to borrow a mop and bucket.

"We'll deal with your punishment later today... after Mr. Hikkling gets back from lunch."

Picking up the pieces of our milk cart crash would be easy. The discipline to follow was another story altogether.

We tapped on the door of Mr. Clifferd's office before cracking it open.

"Hark! Who goes there?" Mr. Clifferd called out in jest.

"Just me and Steeve," I said.

Mr. Clifferd turned around and beheld me in all my glory—chocolate milk and muck in my hair, on my face, and covering me head to toe. He laughed out loud.

"Well, well, get a load of you, my boy! You look like you just fell off the turnip truck."

"Pretty gross, eh?"

"That's an understatement," he said. "I bet there's a good story behind this one."

"We were trying for warp speed!" Crowse said.

"Is that right?" Mr. Clifferd replied with a smile. "And...did you make it?"

"I think so," I said. "At least it sure felt like it."

"So how come it looks like you slid into home base in the middle of a mudslide?" he asked.

"We had a minor accident...right at the end."

"Do tell."

"You know those plants in front of Ms. Schmitts office?" I asked.

"The nice tropical ones," Crowse added.

"I've watered them a time or two," said Mr. Clifferd.

"They sort of got wiped out," I said.

"Must have been some wipeout," said Mr. Clifferd, with a smile.

"You shoulda seen it!" Crowse blurted out.

"And now you're here to tell me the tale of how your mighty attempt at warp speed went awry?"

"Not exactly," I answered. "It's more like, we'd like to borrow your mop and bucket to clean up the aftermath."

"And whose idea was that?"

"Ms. Schmitts, sir," said Crowse.

"Oh my mercy, boys. The old shrew herself."

INTEGRITY

"Yeah, and she was pretty mad," I added.

"No doubt, my young friend, no doubt. And did you tell her what happened?"

"We told her about warp speed," said Crowse..

"And we explained how the milk cart went all crazy at the end," I added.

"Wow boys, this is amazing."

"How come?" I asked.

Mr. Clifferd paused for a moment to gather his thoughts. He took a deep breath, scratched his thinning, grey hair, and sat down on an old, paint-splattered step stool.

"I'm proud of you two," he said.

"Because we hit warp speed?" asked Crowse.

"Well, that's something. But what impresses me, even more, is you two told Ms. Schmitt's the truth about what happened. When you tell the truth, you keep your integrity."

"But what about Ms. Schmitts?" Crowse asked.

"Oh, don't worry about her. I'm sure even she knows you told your truth. Listen, boys, why don't you take this mop and get started, and I'll meet you down there with a couple of garbage bags?"

"Okay, Mr. C. Thanks for helping us out," I said with a smile.

"Yeah, thanks for listening, sir," said Crowse.

"Anytime, gentlemen. Now let's go straighten up the shambles."

As the second wave of the pandemic continues to wash over the world, the effects of the virus are demanding an elevated awareness of our principles, and a sound grip on our chosen morality. We are relying on each other to stay true to our shared responsibilities, and to protect one another by adhering to the recommendations made by infectious disease experts.

To break it down to its simplest expression, we must "say what we do and do what we say." To put it another way, we must always keep our word. As humans, we are an interdependent species. We trust others to honor their commitments, and others expect us to do the same. Integrity is essential in all our interactions. It's crucial that we can count on our fellow members of the human family to keep their promises and to stand by their choices.

This is vital, especially during times of turmoil and uncertainty. We have to know…really know that people will hold fast to their declared commitments. Will everyone honor their word? No, not everyone. There are usually a few rotten apples in every bunch. But that doesn't have to keep us from believing in the fundamental goodness of fellow human beings.

We've all felt the reality of the viral outbreak throughout the planet. In order to contend with the coronavirus, we must up our game in the realms of conduct and morality.

My wife, Nicole, and I love to go to a nearby beach and enjoy a day of sand and sun. We met an elderly gentleman whose home is right beside the beach. His name is Chase. He lives alone, and as of this writing, he's nearly 90-years-old. He is a playful man who always has an interesting story to share from his rich, well-lived life.

When my wife found out Chase is a widower, she decided to "adopt" him. She brings him homemade soup, casseroles, and some of her delicious, made with love baked goodies. She calls him now and then to ask how he's doing. Nicole has made it her responsibility to ensure he's taken care of.

Believe me when I say this, when Nicole commits to doing something, there is no doubt in my mind that she will follow through. Her commitment to her word inspires me. Rain or shine, snow or wind, our old buddy Chase will remain nurtured.

As author and speaker Brené Brown once said, "Integrity is choosing courage over comfort; choosing what is right over what is fun, fast or easy; and choosing to practice our values rather than simply professing them."

Samuel Johnson said, "There can be no friendship without confidence, and no confidence without integrity."

Do as you say.

Keep your word.

Honor your commitments.

Be reliable and trustworthy.

…these are the principles of integrity.

Integrity remains an essential component for humanity to transcend and rise above the challenges of COVID-19. The following phrase (often misattributed to Winston Churchill) captures the critical nature of integrity:

> *"With integrity, nothing else counts.*
> *Without integrity, nothing else counts."*

ABUNDANCE

Brrrrrrrrrrrhhhhhhhh!
The sound of the ferry horn blasted into the warm summer air and straight into our ringing ears.

"Alright!" said Newf. "Boblo Island, here we come!"

"Yeah baby, I can't wait to get on the pirate ship!" said Werrch.

"Me too, man! That's the first ride I'll be jumping on," I replied.

"Yeah? Well, I'm heading straight for the cotton candy!" said Shavy.

Brrrrrrrrrrrhhhhhhhh!

The horn blast announced the steamship was about to disembark.

"Oh boy, oh boy, oh boy!" said Newf as he hopped in place. He couldn't contain himself.

"I've been waiting for this day!"

"It's gonna be a hot one today, too," I answered. "We'll definitely be hitting the log flume!"

"I know what I'll be hitting," Shavy began. "The snow cone machine! Grape, orange, cherry…"

"What about the Wild Mouse?" asked Werrch hollered. "That thing's crazy!"

Brrrrrrrrrrrrhhhhhhhh!

The horn rang out one last time as the ferry pushed off towards the island.

"Can you feel it? We're finally moving!" Shavy shrieked.

The balmy breeze kissed our faces as we peered over the railing and watched the waves of the river lap against the side of the ferry.

Our destination? Bois Blanc Island. Nestled in the middle of the Detroit River, the small island was better known as Boblo Island. It was the home of Boblo Island Amusement Park. No summer would be complete for us without *at least* one visit to this magical isle of delight.

We each had our favorite things about visiting the amusement park. But we all agreed on one thing —a trip to Boblo was always amazing. We looked toward the island in the distance, full of anticipation for all the day had in store for us. We glowed with the thrill of impending adventure and enjoyment.

"I can almost smell the mini-donuts from here!" said Shavy as he salivated.

"I hope they still have those wild swing things! " said Newf. "Those things are nuts!"

"I heard some people went flying off that ride last year. Landed in some big trees nearby," said Werrch.

"Yeah, right. I'm sure that happened, Dingledorf!" replied Newf.

"No, he's right," added Shavy, offering his first non-food-related comment of the day. "I remember that. I heard they couldn't get them down for like a week."

"No way, Jose," said Newf. "That's bonkers!"

"Hey look! I can see the rollercoaster from here!" I said, pointing it out.

"Uggggggghhhh!" moaned Shavy. "I don't like that one. It makes me feel like my stomach is going to pop out of my mouth."

"That's because it's filled with slush puppies and dinky donuts!" teased Newf.

"Don't forget the candy apples!" said Shavy, before falling into a trance. "And the sponge toffee...popcorn...hot pretzels...fried dough..."

"Dude, how can you just *eat* all day long?" asked Werrch.

"It's a gift," Shavy answered with a proud grin on his face.

Brrrrrrrrrrrrhhhhhhhh!

The ferry horn blared again, this time announcing our approaching arrival.

"Hey, you guys remember what happened last year?" I asked.

"You mean with that girl on the Rotor?" Newf asked.

"Yeah, and especially what happened to Alfie!" Werrch said with a laugh.

"I didn't go with you guys last year. What happened?" asked Shavy.

The three of us laughed as Shavy looked at us with eyes desperate for one explanation.

"Well, there was a minor accident," began Newf.

"Yeah, let's just say that Alfie got a little surprise that day," added Werrch.

"More like a big surprise, if you ask me," said Newf.

"C'mon guys, what happened? Tell me already!" said Shavy.

"Ever been on the Rotor?" I asked.

"No way!" said Shavy. "I'd pass out!"

Even though Shavy was a lightweight when it came to rides, he had a point. The Rotor wasn't the gentlest ride in the park. It was a spinning barrel of madness. The floor beneath the riders drops out as the barrel spins. The tremendous g-force pins the passengers to the wall of the whirling drum. Even your cheeks get pulled toward the wall of the rotating cylinder.

Let's just say you had to have a strong stomach to enjoy this adventure. And if your stomach can't handle it, its contents will make a brief exit before covering your face, hair, and the wall surrounding your head. Until the ride slows down, spreading the joy to an unlucky passenger or two.

"So, what happened to Alfie?" asked Shavy.

"Well, he got an unexpected splash in the face," teased Newf.

"Yeah, you know. Like when a bird poops on your head," offered Werrch.

Shavy raised a confused eyebrow.

"Remember that girl we mentioned earlier?" asked Newf. "She kind of lost her lunch."

"Kind of? I'd say she lost it big time!" I added. "And you know what went down next, right?"

"You mean up!" said Newf.

"And sideways!" said Werrch.

"What…what?" Shavy screeched.

"Well…the barf had to go somewhere," I explained.

"And guess whose face it landed on?" Newf asked with a mischievous grin.

"Yep, said Newf. "Right on Alfie's kisser."

"Oh man…that's disgusting!" said Shavy.

"*And* hilarious!" said Newf.

"Yeah, he got blasted with a full load!" said Werrch.

"He's the only one who got soaked. Worse than the girl, even. Leave it to Alfie to have that kind of luck," I said.

"Where is he anyway," asked Shavy.

"Scarred for life," said Werrch.

"You haven't heard Alfie's latest?" asked Newf.

"Uh oh, what did he do this time?"

"He tried an Evel Knievel on his mini-bike and ended up busting his collar bone," said Newf.

"Ouch," said Shavy. "I think he's going to set a world record for mishaps."

"You're not kidding. That guy's a marvel," said Werrch.

"That's why we love him. He's got nine lives," I said.

"I wonder how many he has left?" wondered Shavy.

"Hopefully enough to keep us amused for years to come!" said Newf.

We laughed and nodded, knowing the Alfie Chronicles still held many chapters of entertaining disaster.

As we giggled about the bad luck of our accident-prone friend, we shared a bond of happiness and enjoyment. We knew our buddy would be just fine in due course. And we were ecstatic about sailing towards a day brimming with amusement and abundance.

The island was calling out to us, beckoning to an afternoon the likes of which kids live for—a day of elation and indulgence.

Sensory delights awaited us. Incredible moments that would fill our soul with genuine pleasure.

The summer sun warming our skin. The smell of hot buttered popcorn and corn dogs wafting in the air. The sounds of delighted laughter and joyful screams pulsating throughout the park. Rotating rides. Swirling colors. The tantalizing taste of fountain pop. Sticky saltwater taffy caught in our teeth.

Blue sky. Green foliage. Red tulips. Yellow balloons.

The cool mist from the splash-pad moistening our faces. The rush of racing to the next joyride. The privilege of youth. The arousal of our spirits. The sheer magnificence of life abounding all around us. A never-ending flood of sensations to amplify our experience of being alive.

Indeed, it was a sweet, wondrous day to be alive. A perfect day to soak in all that Boblo Island Amusement Park offered.

When you're a kid, the world seems so enchanting. The world is like a giant amusement park. Kids are spellbound by the astounding array of mysteries and choices. They can't help but love exploration.

What's around this corner? What's behind this door? What's above? What's below? What's this button do?

The more they investigate, the more they discover. The more doors they open, the more doors appear. The more questions they answer, the more new questions come flooding in.

Try this experiment. The next time you go to a grocery store, as that sliding door opens to welcome you in, focus your attention on the astonishing variety available to you. Open your senses to the panoply of options surrounding you. It's a veritable treasure trove of plenty.

If we put someone from 1960 in a time machine and beamed them to a modern-day supermarket, they would be blown away. The produce section alone would be overwhelming. They would find strange fruits and vegetables from around the world. *How did they grow these tomatoes in the middle of the winter? And what the heck does "organic" mean?*

I watched a YouTube video of a man who had been in prison for many years. He filmed himself shopping at a grocery store for the first time. The cereal aisle alone had him nearly speechless as he counted up the varieties of Cheerios available.

We live in a time of abundance. So much is available to us. Do we have the eyes to even see it? The awareness to appreciate it? Or does it all just pass by us like a parade vying for our attention as we stare into the digital screens of our smartphones?

Just think about all the fruits of creativity and invention that we enjoy. The recorded music available for our listening pleasure—most of it available at no cost through the internet. The amazing food and beverages from all parts of the world, ready for us to savor. The books and movies we can dive into and relish—even right from the phones in our pockets. All the different textures you can touch and revel in.

Our extraordinary planet bursts with abundance. It's overflowing with surprises and wonders that boggle the mind. Unfortunately, many of us have gone blind to these things, even if we have 20-20 eyesight. We no longer even *see* them, never mind appreciate them.

So many of us are still alive today, thanks to modern medicine and treatments. For example, if it weren't for the marvel of modern technology, my beautiful wife would no longer be alive. What a blessing!

The gifts of this earth abound everywhere and anywhere. We need only open ourselves to the magnitude of gifts. Any area of life can provide a window to wonder.

For example, think of the animal kingdom. Have you ever seen images of a tardigrade (also called a "water bear")? An axolotl? If not, look them up online and be dazzled.

Think of a less exotic animal: a rabbit. Those floppy ears. Soft fur. That adorable cotton tail bouncing as it hops around, or speeds across an open field. What a magnificent creature!

Think of the canine world—all the varieties and shapes of dogs—the Chihuahua, Newfoundland,

Dachshund ("wiener dog"), the Puli with its mop-like coat, and the varieties of Poodles.

You could make a similar exploration into the world of plants…minerals…weather…the ocean…the solar system. A never-ending supply of fascinating discoveries awaits.

The realities of the pandemic have made people feel like some of the things that make life worth living have vanished. Whether it's going out for dinner at our favorite restaurant, traveling, enjoying a concert or sporting event, or visiting with friends—many of these experiences have gone "on pause." Some are even gone for good—including businesses closed permanently, and loved ones who have passed on. There's a genuine sense of loss and deprivation. Many people want to know when they are going to have these pleasures returned to their lives. As Joni Mitchell sang, *you don't know what you've got 'til it's gone*.

Difficult moments can provide us with the possibility of discovering new or overlooked sources of joy. The present situation can provide us a doorway to a fresh approach to finding the "juice" of the world—opening ourselves to the awesomeness of our existence.

Study a snowflake under a magnifying glass. Gaze upon a spider web. Listen to a songbird. Or the sound of the running water of a creek bed. Smell a wildflower. Stroke the delicate petals of a tiger lily

ABUNDANCE

with your fingertip. Notice all the sights, sounds, smells, tastes, and sensations surrounding us.

We live on a planet engulfed in marvels and miracles. Our planet abounds with more than you could experience in a dozen lifetimes—let alone a single lifetime.

It's time to savor the abundance of life—like exuberant children on a steamship bound for Boblo Island.

BALANCE

"'mon, man. Wake up already!"

This was typical Tops. It was almost noon on a Saturday morning. The sun was shining, the birds were chirping, and there he was, lying lifeless. His bedroom was a dark vault that shut out the rest of the world. When he was in his tomb, he lost all sense of time and space, and disconnected from everything outside it.

"Seriously, Tops. We have to round up Bewdry. We've got some major exploring ahead of us."

"Alright, man. Just give me a minute," he pleaded.

Even though he was drowsy, I knew it wouldn't take him long to get ready. He was a guy who sometimes slept in the same clothes for days. Once he rolled out of bed and put on his smelly sneakers, he'd be ready for action.

That's one thing I loved about Tops—he was always up for an adventure. Usually, all you had to do was come up with a halfway decent idea, suggest it, and he'd be good to go.

Then again, what kid doesn't like a good old-fashioned exploration? A daring venture into the wild was part of the fun of being a young and curious boy. Not quite noon, the day still held much promise—if we could just get going.

"Hurry, man!" I shouted again.

"I'm coming…I'm coming."

The ravine we were to investigate was a five-minute walk from our neighborhood. It was a natural watershed that meandered through our subdivision, winding its way between several houses and flowing into Lake Erie.

This sliver of untainted creation enhanced the Carolinian forest with its sycamore trees, mulberries, and water bugs. Blue herons, black walnut trees, and snapping turtles all found refreshment from the cool waters. I once spotted a red fox taking a cool drink from the edge of the creek.

"Okay, I'm ready," said Tops. He closed behind him the sliding glass door that led to his backyard.

"Perfect. Let's go get Bewdry!"

"You sure he's joining us?"

"Of course. He loves exploring the ravine."

"I don't know man…," Tops said. The puzzled look on my face demanded further explanation.

"Ever since he got that ColecoVision for his birthday, he doesn't even leave his house anymore. All he does is play his video games. Knock on his door. You'll see."

We headed straight over to Bewdry's house, cutting across Mr. Moro's pristine lawn. The shortcut always involved some risk, as Mr. Moro did not take kindly to anyone treading on his luxurious grass carpet. He was the classic crazy neighbor, always yelling at the neighborhood kids and any other trespasser to stay off his property. I never quite understood his such hostile reactions.

Mr. Moro was at least consistent, though. He never even walked on his own grass, either. Why put in the time and effort to cultivate plush, green grass if you aren't going to run across it, roll on it, play on it, wrestle on it, and let it tickle the bottom of your feet and between your toes?

We scurried across the sacred lawn. Fortunately, our breach went undetected. But we had bigger concerns on our minds. We needed to round up our buddy and get on with the exploring.

Bang...bang...bang!

My knuckles knocked with conviction on Bewdry's front door.

"Hey, Bewdry! You in there?"

We stood and waited for a reply.

Bang...bang...bang!

"Hey, man! Where are you?" I asked, louder than before.

Again, we stood by, waiting for an answer that did not come. This wasn't like Bewdry. He always answered the door when we came to call, especially when we already made plans for the day.

"Let me try," Tops offered.

Bang...bang...bang!

"Hey, Bewdry! It's Tops. You coming outside, or what?"

Silence. We looked at each other with disappointment. The least he could do is answer the darn door. That's just common courtesy.

Suddenly, we heard movement inside. Footsteps approaching, then the sound of the door unlocking. The door slowly creaked open to reveal Bewdry's mom, standing in the doorway with a concerned look on her face. She *never* answered the door when we came calling, and yet there she was, looking directly at us.

"Halo boyssh," she said in her distinct Dutch accent. "Mikel ish not goingk out today."

"We planned this last week...," I began.

"Yesh. But he's not goingk out," she insisted.

"How come?" asked Tops.

"He hashn't been out in days," she answered with sadness in her voice. I was glad Tops had tipped me off about the ColecoVision. Otherwise, I would have thought he was gravely ill or worse.

"All he wants to do is play that schtupid video games," she said. Tops elbowed me.

"Has he gone outside at all? Like to ride his bike, or cut the grass?" I asked.

"Nutting. He doeschn't even come to eat at the table."

"Well, can you at least ask him to come to the door so we can talk to him?" I asked. "Maybe when he sees us here, ready to go, he'll change his mind.

Mrs. Bewdry shook her head with a big frown on her face.

"He won't even leave hish room." she replied. "I've tried…but he's too dishtracted."

Both Tops and I looked at each other with disappointment. We felt like we had lost a friend.

It was disturbing to witness. The person I used to go tree climbing with…who helped me build snow forts…was now mesmerized by the flashing graphics and hypnotic sounds of a gaming console. We'd heard of cases like this with other kids. We've heard stories of how video games had enthralled and stupefied kids, casting a strange spell that changed who they were and how they behaved. The result was a loss of interest in the outside world. The slow pace of the natural world just could not compete with the addictive gameplay.

The pandemic has caused many of us to spend more time indoors. This trend has coincided with an increase in "screen time," including video games (though likely not much ColecoVision these days), television, movies, or social media.

Experts suggest some people spend eight, ten, or even twelve-plus hours in front of their various devices. The end results of these behavioral choices? Sedentary lives, lived indoors and disconnected from the natural world.

Human beings are physical creatures who have interacted with and explored the environment for eons. We benefit from fresh air, flora and fauna, and tapping into the endless energy of the ecosystem. The more time we spend outdoors, the more we feel invigorated and full of life.

Children flourish and thrive when provided the opportunity to play outside. The more they explore and use their imaginations, the greater their well-being. Kids love playing on the grass, splashing in the water, climbing trees, and rolling on a sandy beach.

Ever watch youngsters frolicking at a local park or playground? Ever witness them horsing around with sticks and rocks, or stomping in a mud puddle? They revel in the magic of the natural world, whether they are city dwellers or country folk.

Left to their own devices (electronics excluded!), children connect with the trees, the insects, and the rain—the natural splendors that inspire us, sustain us and infiltrate our souls. They love to interact with the natural world. Think of the young child who, to the chagrin of their pragmatic parents, wades into a pond wearing their Sunday's best. The water is *there*, and it's *calling* them, *enticing* them. Children will play in the snow with abandon until their fingers, toes, and noses are practically frostbitten. They'll roll in the mud like it's a spa treatment. They'll take a dip in the ocean, then roll on the beach—becoming one with the sand. They experience the *joie de vivre* in a physical, tactile way, with little concern for clean clothes, hands, or faces.

I suspect we all have memories of a time when we felt caught up in a love affair with our magnificent planet. Who hasn't delighted in at least some of the vast, innumerable blessings the earth provides us?

Take a moment and ask yourself: what are some of your favorite aspects of the great outdoors? What places or sights have filled you with awe? What landscapes or vistas have taken your breath away?

You need not have traveled the world to answer this question. No matter where you live on this planet, there is a sky above you. There is a sun. A moon. Vegetation. Animals and insects. Water. Weather.

What moves you? Is it the sunshine? A gentle breeze? The majesty of the mountains? A soaring hawk? A pigeon in the park? An ant on a window sill? Is it a fresh strawberry or tomato plucked off the vine? The scent of honeysuckle or pine needles? The gritty feel of sand in your toes? The rejuvenating jolt when jumping into a nearby river, lake, or pond?

Whatever it might be, consider yourself privileged to experience these wonders. And the next time you have an opportunity to connect with the natural world—even by simply stepping outside for a mindful moment— I invite you to experience it with all of your senses awake. Simply vibrate with receptivity to the aliveness surrounding you. Breathe it all in, drink it all in, soak it all in.

With all this talk of the natural world, you might wonder if I'm an advocate for returning to cave dweller times, or to our hunter/gatherer origins. While I respect those who have gone before us, I also appreciate modern technology. It's served us in many positive ways. For example, without technology, you would likely not be reading this printed (or digital) book. Before the printing press, copies of important writings were produced by monks who copied them by hand. Technology has allowed us to develop as a species. It has lengthened our lives and opened doors of understanding and mastery that our ancestors could never have imagined. Yet, these benefits come with costs and risks that some of us—like poor Bewdry—are not prepared to handle.

How can we embrace the best aspects of modern life without losing ourselves? How can we embrace technology and maintain a connection with the natural world and our roots?

The question is the answer.

That might sound like a koan, a riddle, or a clever saying. However, it is simpler than it appears. The question—that is, asking the question, caring about it, contemplating it—is the door to the answer.

Ultimately, the answer we find will involve balance. But the specific balance point will be different for each of us. If we live within that question, however—regularly assessing and reassessing our balance—we'll be less likely to fall off-balance. And when we do, we'll re-balance quicker.

It is vital that we find our own optimal combination of scientific savvy and primal awareness. Spending most of your time staring at a screen is not a recipe for creating a healthy, prosperous society. We must expand our ability to embrace new advances while staying mindful of the natural world.

Remember this…

The next time you witness a rainbow or a sunset…

Or go tobogganing, or fishing…

When you next smell a bonfire…

Or a rose in your garden…

When you next touch your child's hair…

Or a snowflake kisses your nose...

Recall these are all blessings of the natural world. They are artifacts from the Creator's own hand, made with the finest expertise and technical precision. And they come from an infinite catalog. (Ever seen a photograph of a snowflake up close? Recall that every single snowflake that ever floated from the sky has a unique design—it will blow your mind!)

Let's stay ever mindful of both the world of innovative technological advancement, and the natural world of astounding beauty and brilliance.

Let's take a balanced approach that embraces and respects both worlds with wisdom and reverence.

With our eyes on the sky and feet on the ground, let's dance through both worlds with force, elegance, and grace.

CHOICE

"Gee, nice going Chris. You just cost us ten house points." Lawrie looked at me with daggers in her eyes.

"We put in all this effort to earn them, and then you turn around and lose them for us," she added.

"Hey, that's not true," I said. "I put numbers on the board, too…sometimes."

"Trust me, buddy, you lose far more than you ever gain," said Lawrie.

In my defense, I took part in both surrendering and earning those precious house points. Some days, though, I lost them as fast as I made them.

The school introduced the house point system to reward and punish students based on their behavior. When a student did something that pleased a teacher, they scored points for their team, or "house." When a classmate upset or annoyed a teacher, the house lost points. I doubt they used the term "social engineering," but that's what it amounted to. I had a knack for both winning and losing points in droves. But I'm not sure any of it made me a better-behaved student.

The name of my house was Algonquin, after an aboriginal tribe in the Ottawa River valley. The competing houses were Huron, Ojibwa, and Iroquois. They assigned each student to a tribe.

The rivalry to attain points for one's house could get intense. When a kid would lose points for their house, the reaction would lead you to believe they had committed a criminal offense. The teachers took full advantage of this social disapproval, using it as leverage to ensure cooperative conduct and submission. The sharp, derisive looks one would get for losing those sacred tribal points was at once amusing and unnerving.

When you think about it, the house points were an ingenious system. The teachers created them out of thin air, by decree. The points weren't worth anything tangible. They weren't redeemable. No amount of points would garner treats or extra privileges. *A totalitarian's dream.* It reminds me of the concept of bottling water and persuading everyone to pay a premium for it when it's available from the faucet at home.

"We're trying to win first place, Knucklehead. You keep moving us in the wrong direction." Lawrie wouldn't quit. Her tenacity attracted other students to join in.

"Yeah, you dumbkof!" said Jojo. "You're costing us big time, Forman."

"C'mon, give me a break," I pleaded with the growing mob. "I can't help it if Mrs. Grubb doesn't appreciate the distinct pleasure of twacking."

"You know twacking isn't allowed, and getting caught means an automatic deduction," said Lawrie.

"I know, but man, his lobes were just crying out for a proper twack. How can you blame me?"

If you're unfamiliar with the term, allow me to bring you up to speed. A *twack* is a crisp flick to the back of a person's ear lobes, delivered with a firm snap of one's middle finger. For the twackers among us, anyone with large, protruding ear lobes offered an almost irresistible temptation. Those soft, juicy lobes hanging off the sides of the head *begged* for a twacking. The twack was delivered from behind, resulting in surprise and a mild sting. A twack was most successful when it garnered an annoyed reaction.

Ah, how I miss delivering a solid *twack*. To what could I compare that moment of satisfaction? Even if it was a bit of a dirty trick, the twack was good, clean fun. It was one of the most awesomely annoying things about being an adolescent boy.

"That twack right there just lost us ten points," Jojo stated.

As if I didn't know that already.

"But just look at those babies. They were calling out for some loving attention."

How could they not see this logic? And where were my fellow twackers to back me up, just when I needed them most?

"Just leave Tyller's ears alone!" Lawrie insisted. "Look at how red they are now."

"That's the whole point!" I pleaded. "I always say, *if the ears aren't bright, you didn't twack 'em right.*"

"Oh, grow up already, will you?" she muttered.

I don't know what it was with girls at my school, but somehow they just never appreciated the enjoyment we boys derived from inflicting mild discomfort on our classmates. Whether it was a good wedgie, a dandelion butter face, an icy snow wash, or a lovely twacking, delivering an unexpected bite of unpleasantness was part of the guy code that most of us young bucks lived by.

Twacking transcended the categories of right or wrong. To us, it was a morally neutral act. It was a choice to inflict a moderate amount of annoyance and elicit a reaction. *Stimulus and response. Action, reaction.*

The intention was playful provocation, done in a spirit of lighthearted mischief. Perhaps it wasn't the most considerate or noble of gestures. But there was no ill will intended. No one got seriously hurt. And even if it cost some house points, it was worth it. *The price of freedom.*

What is it about simply making our own choices that people are sometimes afraid of? Is it the fear of not being accepted? The dread of reprisal or punishment? The angst of potential catastrophe or failure? Losing "social credit"?

It is only when we *choose freely* that we can *live freely*. The constraints of social norms and societal conventions can limit our capacity to honor our own intuition and make the decisions that feel right to us.

It's essential to make our own choices. We must choose our path and own it. Of course, every decision has a price, especially when it involves other people. That's just how it goes in human society. The key is to be aware of the power of free will and to exercise that potential with responsibility and sincerity. We are tribal beings. If you stop and think about it, some form of "house points" is always in effect, whether or not we realize it. (I'd rather skip the points and embrace the twack.)

A big debate in our culture right now involves euthanasia. In some ways, euthanasia represents the freedom of choice to its fullest degree. There are many opinions on this issue, and many factors to consider when pondering this matter. (This includes the rights of those who—perhaps because of their mental or physical state—may face euthanasia not by their own choice, but at the insistence of family members or medical professionals.)

The question comes down to where we stand on the freedom to choose our own fate, even for life or death. We all have different thoughts and feelings concerning who has the ultimate say in this monumental determination, and I'm not here to tell you what to believe. I think, however, if you haven't thought about this question, it's one worth pondering. Sometimes considering extreme examples can help bring clarity.

What do you think? Should we have the right to choose between our own life or death? Your response will be tied to your belief about the meaning and consequences of freedom of choice. Your beliefs on what happens after we die may also factor in. I think it's important to look at the question with honesty, setting aside concerns about social repercussions of coming down on the "wrong side of the issue."

COVID-19 has pushed us to make decisions in areas related to our morality. It has thrust us into uncharted territory, forcing us to pick from a multitude of difficult options. Some have encountered family members or close friends with opposing opinions. Relationships have splintered or even ended over it.

Ideally, we will make such arduous evaluations with goodwill and a loving spirit. If we bring these intentions to our exploration, and go beyond anxiety and despair, we will land in more thoughtful territory.

CHOICE

As I write these words, my wife is contending with a serious health challenge that has left her weak, dizzy, and confused. She has fallen several times, resulting in bruises to her forehead and eyes. She looks a bit like she's just gone a few rounds in a boxing ring. I am now faced with the decision to either take her to the hospital in Windsor, Ontario and have her admitted, or to keep her home and do my best to care for her on my own.

Under normal circumstances, I would have taken her in right away to receive care from the amazing health care workers in the Ontario medical system. However, because of the virus and the resulting overload at the hospitals, I'm apprehensive about placing her in such a volatile environment.

Sometimes we all have to make tough choices in life. Even though I face a heavy dilemma, I am doing so without fear or desperation. Of course, I will consider possible outcomes. But ultimately, I will choose freely. Love and awareness will inform whatever path I take.

As I continue to contemplate the risks involved in choosing either Door #1, or Door #2, (or perhaps a Door #3 or #4 that I have yet to discover), I resolve to remain calm and clearheaded, knowing that I will make this selection straight from the heart without doubt or distress.

I am sure there are many people out there in the world right now that are in similar or even more troublesome circumstances. Whatever they end up choosing, I hope they do so with trust and faith as their guides—trust in their soul, and faith in their conscience.

Our lives are filled with predicaments where the best move is not obvious. If we place confidence in our intuition and focus on our internal compass, we can conquer our perplexity.

Just as I did way back in the days of my youth, I will continue to place my hope and conviction in the inner voice that always knows what is best for our well-being.

And, for what it's worth, as much as I would still enjoy a good *twack* every now and again, I've freely chosen to set that behavior aside.

LOVE

"**H**ey Forman, did you hear what happened to Mr. Hikkling?" Goz asked me.

"No, but let me guess, whatever it was, he blamed it on me?" I replied.

"No, man, not this time," said Goz. He looked concerned; it worried me.

"What is it? You look like you just saw a ghost."

"We just might…if he doesn't make it," said Goz.

"What do you mean by that?" I asked as a lump formed in my throat.

"He had a heart attack."

"For real?"

"Totally. My mom knows his wife. Last night she told her he's in the hospital."

"Woah, that sounds serious!" I said.

"Could be. I'm surprised it didn't happen sooner."

"What do you mean?"

"You know how he gets sometimes. That guy blows his top multiple times per week," said Goz.

"Yeah, and it's usually blowing in my direction."

"Well, you *do* push his buttons, Chris."

"Not on purpose!" I insisted.

"Either way, he has a tough job."

"With me as one of the students he's responsible for, I guess I have to agree," I admitted.

I thought of my many run-ins with Mr. Hikkling over the months and years. Goz was right. I could get him so wound up sometimes that you would swear he could put me in a catapult and launch me to the moon.

I had a strange knack for getting under his skin, eliciting steam from his ears. We weren't best buddies by any stretch, but I never wished him harm. I just wished he'd relax and consider my side of the story. The thought of him dying made me sad and put a knot in my stomach. As one of his top sources of stress, I felt somewhat responsible for his predicament.

Did I push the guy over the edge? Maybe I could have tried to appreciate his point of view? If he died from this, would it be my fault?

"Hey man, you okay?" asked Goz.

"Yeah, I'm alright, I guess. I just feel bad. You know?"

"Yeah, me, too," said Goz. "Let's hope he gets better."

"You think he'll make it?"

"My mom thinks so. She said he's pretty young for this to happen, and he'll put up a good fight to recover."

"If he puts up half the effort he does in chasing me down, I like his chances."

Goz laughed at my comment.

"Hey, do you think Mr. C. knows anything about it?" I asked.

"Maybe. You should go find out."

"I'll ask him if you'll come with me," I said.

I always liked Goz. I looked to him for guidance and encouragement. Some people may have called him an "old soul". He was kind, intelligent, and exuded a calm, wise presence that made me feel that all was well with the world. Of all my friends, Goz was the most dependable. If I ever had doubts or fears, all I had to do was share them with Goz. He always seemed to know what to say to ease my mind and make me feel better.

"Hey, Mr. C! You in here?" Goz called into the boiler room.

"Hark! Who goes there?"

"Tis Mr. Forman and me," Goz replied with mock formality. Mr. Clifferd came around the corner.

"To what do I owe this pleasure, my good friends?"

"We wondered if you heard about Mr. Hikkling?" I asked.

"Yes, my boy. I heard the unfortunate news." Goz and I stood before him. We weren't even sure what else to say.

"How you boys doing with the news?" he asked, making eye contact with each of us as he spoke.

"Okay, I guess," said Goz. "We're just not sure… what it all means."

"Well…," began Mr. Clifferd with a thoughtful look on his face. "I suppose it could mean several things. It all depends on how you look at it."

"What do you mean?" I asked.

"Well, my good men, it rests on how you feel about the power of unconditional love. And what you believe happens after we die."

"Whoa, Mr. C,….that sounds pretty heavy," said Goz.

"I agree with you. In fact, I'd say it's the heaviest subject I know. It concerns the two ultimate questions we all need to ask ourselves."

"What questions are those?" I asked.

"Well, my friends, it's like this…," he began before collecting his thoughts. "When one considers matters of life and death, it's essential to remember the one universal truth that rises above all others."

"And what is that, sir?" asked Goz.

"It's the undeniable fact that the most powerful force in the world is unconditional love," said the janitor.

LOVE

"Unconditional love, sir?" I questioned. I could think of lots of candidates for the most powerful force in the world—and love was not among them.

"That's right, boys. A love that knows no bounds. Has no limits. A love that compels you to give everything you have and all that you are to honor its existence," said Mr. Clifferd.

"Wow," said Goz. "Have you ever felt that kind of love?"

"Indeed I have, my boy. In fact, I still experience it daily."

"Every day?" I asked.

"Absolutely. I feel it everywhere I go. Especially when I think about my beautiful beloved bride," he said. He looked down, adding, "May she rest in peace." I watched a small tear forming in the corner of his left eye.

"Your wife…died?" asked Goz with hesitation.

"Sadly so," he answered. "Let me tell you boys, if there ever was a story of unconditional love, it's the one I wrote with my amazing and unforgettable Grace."

"That was her name? Grace?" I asked.

"Not only was it her name—it was everything she embodied and expressed," said Mr. Clifferd, controlling a slight crack in his voice.

"May I ask what happened to her, sir?" asked Goz.

"Strangely enough, my young friends, she died from the same thing Mr. Hikkling is battling right now. A heart attack."

"I'm so sorry," said Goz.

"For a long time, my heart felt like it was broken, too," he said. "I suffered to my very core. Then one day, I had a thought that changed my perspective. I realized just how lucky I had been to experience such a love."

"Wow, you really loved her a lot, didn't you, Mr. C.?" asked Goz.

"I still do, my boy. She will always be a part of my very soul. The difference now is that instead of mourning her death and walking around half-dead myself, I'm celebrating her life and living each day fully alive."

"Wow sir, that's amazing," I said. "I hope one day Goz and I will find a love like that."

"Me, too, my friends," Mr. Clifferd replied with tenderness. "There is nothing more wonderful, or more fulfilling, than unconditional love. It lasts forever and survives even death."

The world has irrevocably changed because of COVID-19. The pandemic introduced humanity to new challenges and demands. Will we rise to the occasion? Will we exit the pandemic with a newfound understanding of how to thrive in a changed environment?

Can we adapt to the new circumstances? Will we embrace unconditional love? Will we commit to doing whatever it takes to look after all our brothers and sisters in the human family?

Will we address the heartbreaking pain and suffering that is a part of the daily lives of so many? Will we give everything we have to make sure our human family feels loved and cared for?

As I ponder these questions, my wife is contending with a major flare-up in her ongoing struggle with blood cancer. She's been in the hospital for over a week now. The thought of her anguish and discomfort makes me feel distraught and helpless.

Believe me, if I could, I would trade places with her in a heartbeat. I don't know what it's like to be a parent and watch your children suffer. I don't know what it feels like to send your kids into the new world the virus cast us into.

I do know this. I love my wife. I love her with a depth and power that I have never before known. She has taught me how to open my heart with a devotion that knows no limits. I would do anything for her at this moment, including sacrificing my own life. I'm not sure if that's what unconditional love is, but it just may be as close as I will ever get in this lifetime.

Have you seen the film (or read the book), *The Notebook*? It's a romantic love story about a young couple that stays together despite many obstacles. The two lovers grow old together. As a senior, the wife suffers from dementia. She hardly remembers who she is. She has forgotten all the wonderful experiences she shared with her beloved husband.

Now and then, however, something sparks a memory. In these moments, she and her husband share a brief glimpse of their shared love story. The husband awaits these flashes with enduring patience and love. What a love this man must have felt, given his faithfulness, despite only brief moments of mutual connection. Watching the film, your heart both soars and breaks at the same time.

The pandemic has unleashed a torrent of emotions upon all of humanity. Some people haven't been able to see their loved ones in person for months on end. Some have lost family members without a chance to say goodbye. Even funeral services have been put on hold or had attendance restricted in many places. Some of the related stories on the evening news are gut-wrenching. The pain is so vivid. I feel the agony, grief, and sorrow.

This virus is tearing our lives apart in different ways. There is only one way we are going to weather this storm and rise to a new state of being. We face a harsh reality that only one force can remedy. This moment calls out for a love that is great enough to

LOVE

expand our hearts and encircle the entire human family. No one excluded, no one left behind.

Steeping souls in a spirit of kindness will ensure a successful continuation of our species. There's no more time for "us" and "them" anymore. We must realize that love is for *giving* rather than *getting*. (Not to worry, though, if we love, love will return to us). If we care for each other unconditionally, we can rise above any pandemic. Any ordeal. Any disaster. We can let friendship and ardor serve as our guides.

Just look at what our frontline healthcare workers have done since the start of the crisis. They have risked their health and their lives to help those in distress. They are tired, uncomfortable, burnt-out. Yet, they do their utmost to make sure people are being taken care of and loved. What an inspiration for us all!

The frontline healthcare workers show us all what it takes to care with everything you've got. We are so blessed to have these incredible individuals willing to face the dangers of COVID-19 and the hazards and stress of watching others suffer.

These amazing individuals run into a burning building every time they don their scrubs. When I see the sacrifices they make, it fills me with immense pride to be human. This is humanity at its best, and we owe them our heartfelt gratitude and recognition. They need our support now and will surely need it once the crisis has passed, too.

Together, we can do this. We can stretch our wings and find a higher way of experiencing life and growing our capacity for love.

Virus or no virus, love will help us rise above any challenges with dignity and grace.

THE FUTURE

The music of Alice Cooper's "School's Out" blasted out from the school's archaic P.A. system.

Cooper's rebellious words rang throughout the classroom as we all belted out the lyrics at the top of our lungs.

"Yeah, we made it, baby!" yelled Alfie.

"School is out—forever!" said Schmig Al.

"You know it!" Alfie said. "I'm joining the carnival!"

"You're what?" I asked.

"You know, the guys with the gold teeth who travel from town to town," Alfie explained. "I'm signing up, big time. I'm going to run the Tilt-A-Whirl!"

"That's awesome!" said Schmig Al. "Maybe I'll go with you."

"What job would you do?" Alfie asked.

"Duh, that's easy," said Schmig Al. "I'll run the hot dog cart."

"Ha ha! Good luck with that!" I said. "You'll eat all the inventory."

"I'm with you, Schmig!" Shavy said. "We can be partners. You sell the dogs, and I'll sell the dinky donuts. We'll make a fortune together!"

"Get real, Shavy. Between you and Schmig, they'll be nothing but burping and a sign that says, 'Sorry folks...we're out of dogs and dinkies,'" said Newf.

"Yeah, you two eating machines will be out of business after your first day!" said Jonny.

"Whatever, bucko!" Shavy countered. "You'll see. We're gonna be famous."

"You'll be famous, alright," said Jef. "Two boys' bellies explode at carnival. News at eleven."

"For sure!" Dooey added. "They'll be guts and donuts spraying everywhere!"

We all laughed at the thought of the contents of Schmig and Shavy's stomachs decorating the fairgrounds.

We couldn't contain our excitement. School was out for the next couple of months. That sweet, glorious season of summer had arrived. The anticipation filled us with delight.

Swimming. Baseball. Watermelon. Root beer. Shorts. Bare feet in the grass.

The magic of the heat and the sun.

THE FUTURE

The carefree, long days of sprinklers, tree-climbing, and driftwood fires.

The pure pleasures of kite flying, hot dogs, and blowing soap bubbles.

When you're a kid, the summer is wondrous and enchanting. We couldn't wait for the festivities to begin.

"I'm trying out for the travel baseball team this year!" said Werrch.

"I'm going to ride my dirt bike!" said Crowse.

"I'm going vine-swinging," said Nak. "Maybe do some camping, too."

"That sounds great!" said Jonny. "I love being outside in the summer."

"Not me," said Boobee. "I like air conditioning and reruns of *What's Happening!!*"

"You would!" Jef said. "That's why you're still pasty white in September."

"So what? Just think of how nice my skin will look when I'm older," said Boobee.

We all laughed together.

We each had our own favorite aspect of the beautiful season of summer. There's a natural high in anticipating the season. The summer offers a marvelous treasure in a kid's life—lazy, hazy days of easygoing, feel-good freedom.

"Hey, Forman. Are you going to say goodbye to Mr. C.?" asked Crowse.

"Of course. You coming with me?"

"Wish I could. My mom's picking me up in five minutes."

"What about you, Boobee. You joining me?"

"No can do, Forman. I need to get home and check on my turtles."

"Go see him by yourself, Chris. You're his favorite, anyway," said Jef.

"You think so?"

"No doubt. You've spent more time in the boiler room than the rest of us combined," said Newf.

"Yeah, you spent so much time there, you should have been on the payroll," said Shavy.

"Yeah, I can't tell you how many times Mr. C.'s been there for me."

"I can," said Werrch. "How about a million?"

We all laughed. Exaggeration aside, he was right in that no one spent as much 'quality time' in the company of Mr. C. as me.

He was like a big brother, a father, and a master mentor, all wrapped in one. Mr. Clifferd was a true teacher, a guide, and a friend.

"Okay, guys. I'm off to see the Wonderful Clifferd of Oz. Have a wicked summer, boys!"

"You, too!" said Alfie. "Call me when you want to go fishing…or inner-tubing," he added, brimming with possibilities.

"Sounds good, buddy. See you guys!" I called out as I headed down the hall.

This would be the last time I'd see Mr. C. until school started back up in the fall. I thought about

THE FUTURE

what I might say to him. He had done so much for me over the past year, and I wanted to thank him. He had been there through the good, the bad, and the grisly. Whatever injustice or predicament I encountered, he always had my back. He was my confidante and hero. Who would have imagined such kindness and wisdom would emerge from the confines of a simple custodian's office? Of all places, how could it be that the boiler is the one room in the entire school where I learned the most?

Bang! Bang! Bang!

I rapped my knuckles on the heavy metal door of Mr. C.'s office.

"You in there, sir?"

The door creaked open. Mr. Clifferd popped his head out to greet me.

"Enough with the 'sir' business already!" he said. "Am I that old already?" he asked with a pretend angry face that morphed into his familiar wide grin.

"Hey, Mr. C. I just came to say goodbye before the summer break."

"You did, eh?" he asked. "Well, come right on in. And let's hear what's on your mind before you head home," he said as he opened the door and gestured for me to step into his office.

"Have a seat, laddie," he said in his customary welcoming way. "You must be pretty excited about all the upcoming adventures."

"You know it!" I answered.

"Well, my young friend, that kind of excitement is what life is all about," he said. "We are here to enjoy all the amazing thrills of life."

"I hear you, Mr. C.," I replied. "I can't wait to get out into the woods and explore."

"If anyone can cook up an interesting time, it's you, my young friend," he said with a chuckle.

"How about you, Mr. C.? What are your plans for the summer?"

"Funny you should ask," he said with a grin. "I just booked a trip to go see my brother way up in Northern Ontario."

"What are you going to do up there?" I asked.

"We're going to build a brand new deck for our family's cottage," he shared with excitement.

"Oh man, that sounds like a lot of work to me, Mr. C."

"Not to me, my boy. I enjoy working with my hands, especially when I'm building something my family and I will enjoy for years to come. Besides, when you love your work, it can feel like play."

"That makes sense," I said. "You sure are a hard worker, Mr. C."

"Oh, don't you worry about me, son. I may be an old geezer, but I've got some life left in me still. There will be plenty of time for this old dog to have some fun up north," he said with a twinkle in his eye.

"What will you do for fun when you're not working on the deck?"

"Well, my boy, it's like this. If there's a swimming hole, I'm jumping in it. If there's a fish, I'm catching it. If there's a boat, I'm rowing it. And if there's a beer, I'm drinking it!"

"Right on!" I cheered.

"Hold on...did I say beer? I meant *lemonade*, son, *lemonade*," he clarified. "If there's a *lemonade*, I'm drinking it."

"Of course, *lemonade*!" I said, going along with the ruse.

As Mr. Clifferd described his summer plans, I saw the boy inside the man. The janitor's youthful, adventurous spirit burst forth into the steamy space of the boiler room. With fervor and joy on his glowing face, I could feel his contagious enthusiasm and zest for life. It filled the expanse of that extraordinary magical office.

Mr. C. was full of life. He overflowed with love and elation about being alive. It was moving to feel his passion and energy.

He reminded me of...*me*.

No wonder he was the one adult I connected with at the entire school.

"That sounds amazing, Mr. C! Just be sure you don't drink too much of that *lemonade*," I said.

"All things in moderation, my boy. Including *lemonade*."

"Well, it sure sounds like we're both going to have an amazing summer," I said.

"Most definitely. I look forward to hearing all your tales of glory when I see you again in the fall," he said with a wink.

"Me, too!" I said. "And I want to hear about your new deck. And the swimming holes. And the fish you catch!" I said. Mr. Clifferd sat there smiling at me. I wanted to ask him a question, but I hesitated for a few moments. Finally, I came out with it.

"Mr. C., could I give you a hug?" He stood up with a smile and stretched his arms wide. I jumped up from my chair and threw my arms around him.

"Thanks for always being there for me, Mr. Clifferd." The intensity of my own emotions surprised me, and I fought back tears.

"You are most welcome, Chris. It is always an honor when you come knocking. And *thank you*—for having the courage to speak your mind, along with the willingness to reflect and grow."

I could hardly believe my ears. No adult had ever said anything like that to me. Then again, Mr. Clifferd said a lot of things I'd never heard from adults. I felt *seen*, *cherished*, and *appreciated*. Not just in that moment—but *always* when in his presence.

"You have yourself an incredible summer, my boy," he said as I pushed the door open to leave. I turned and looked back into his assuring eyes one last time before my summer vacation officially began.

THE FUTURE

Consider for a moment the following questions.

Where is humanity headed?

What does the future hold in store for us?

What do we envision and desire as our destiny as a species?

Is it possible that we can choose our fate?

Do we have the ability to push past the bounds of our prospects?

What do you think? I believe that there is no doubt about it—we have the power to determine humankind's outcome. The first step is to awaken to that truth. It starts with realizing we are the authors and designers of our future. We are the creators poised to craft our evolution.

Our astounding powers of imagination and the resilient human spirit will rule the day when we embrace our capacity to influence our destiny. We are the captains of this awesome vessel we call life. If we so choose, we can call the shots as we sail forward into the great unknown.

What is the best way to steer the ship? Where are the most favorable waters with the best conditions for sailing?

If Mr. C. were here today and we posed such questions to him, I imagine he would take a deep breath, ease back in his rickety wooden chair and beam with boundless love and optimism. He would reach down deep into his soul and renew our faith in each other by affirming the human spirit. He would remind us of who we *really* are, and the immense power we wield in our kismet.

It's our responsibility to realize our profound connection to one another. We can rise to new heights with our capacity to love our human family without conditions.

Our ability to express generosity, to share our bounty, will lift all beings to higher security and satisfaction. If we commit to cooperate with one another with mutual respect, we can climb new peaks of prosperity.

If we can be open and honest with our brothers and sisters in the world, there is no question we can attain unimagined levels of achievement and fulfillment.

We live on one of the most wonderful, abundant planets in the universe. We can bask in the ample waters of joy and wonder that this bountiful earth offers us all.

We can conquer any challenge with wisdom and heartfelt love. We can overcome any hardship and rise above any pandemic or other obstacle cast upon our shoulders.

THE FUTURE

It's up to every one of us to respect the precious sanctity of life. It's in our collective hands to harness both nature and technology and make the world a better place for generations to come.

Let's make a collective vow to honor the magnificent gift of life. Let this promise serve as a sign of gratitude for all that we savor.

Let's all unite in our shared hope for a promising future and an unlimited adventure, taking us places of which we may only dream.

Let's all follow the wisdom and love expressed within the lessons of these pages, and make Mr. C. proud of what we have decided to *Be* together.

ABOUT CHRIS FORMAN

Chris Forman is a transformational speaker and author who inspires his audiences to awaken as individuals and members of the human family.

Chris is the Founder & CEO of Personal Sage, and the creator of the forthcoming video series, *True Wealth: A 30-Day Adventure to Discover Your Inner Riches*. Through his Personal Sage Coaching, he provides 1:1 inspiration and insight to ALL who are ready to take the next step on their journey to transformation.

A professional bartender for over twenty-five years, Chris has gleaned uncommon wisdom from conversations with thousands of diverse patrons, leading to deep insights into the human condition.

He lives in Leamington, Ontario, Canada, with his beloved bride, Nicole.

LET'S STAY CONNECTED

Thanks so much for reading *Mr. C. & Me*.

I have lots of exciting plans and projects in store for the coming months, including the release of my video series.

Let's connect so you can stay in the loop, and I can support you on YOUR journey as well!

 chris@personal-sage.com

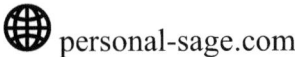 personal-sage.com

 @personal_sage

 fb.com/personalsage

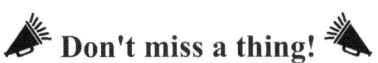 **Don't miss a thing!**

Sign-up for my newsletter at personal-sage.com and you'll get the **latest developments** here at *Personal Sage*, including **exclusive access** to **special offers**.

A Free Gift for You!

As a thank you for purchasing this book, I'd like to offer you a FREE audio download of my keynote presentation, based on the content of *True Wealth*.

To claim your free gift, go to:

personal-sage.com/audio

ALSO AVAILABLE IN EBOOK & PAPERBACK

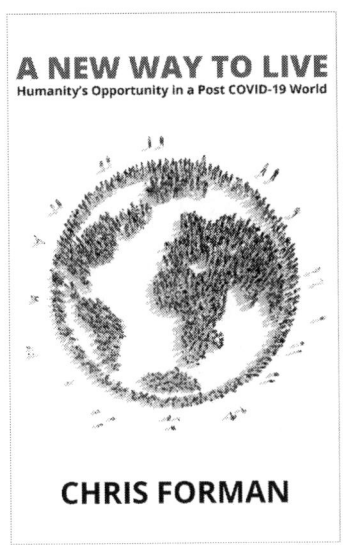

Chris Forman's first book *A New Way To Live* issues a powerful clarion call for humanity to find a new approach to living together on planet earth in the wake of COVID-19.

Despite widespread wishes to cling to the past, life is not going back to "the way it was" before the pandemic. Will the pandemic be another blow that fractures and divides us? Or will we let it serve as a wake-up call to find our way back to truly sustainable lifestyles and relationships?

With solutions rooted in balance, empathy and love, Chris Forman challenges readers to usher in a new way of being—an evolution of humanity

**Are you rich?
Fabulously wealthy?
Blessed beyond belief?**

Yes, you are! You just might not know it yet. *True Wealth* offers you the opportunity to claim your rightful fortune! *Make no mistake:* this is not a book about financial literacy, savvy investing, or thrifty spending. *It's not about money at all.*

True Wealth is about the most valuable things in life that money cannot buy, fix, or replace—the *real* Jewels of our existence on the planet.

Chris Forman will lead you to your forgotten fortune and teach you how to tap your personal vault of riches and access the abundant inheritance you deserve. You'll discover and embrace each of the Twelve Jewels of True Wealth.

Come along for a tour of the very best things in life, conveyed through sage wisdom and delightful true stories that will awaken your heart and stir your soul. Meet outrageous characters who will have you laughing out loud. Rediscover yourself and renew your faith in humanity—all while growing richer and richer.

Manufactured by Amazon.ca
Bolton, ON